Hugh Poyntz Malet

Lost links in the Indian mutiny

Hugh Poyntz Malet

Lost links in the Indian mutiny

ISBN/EAN: 9783337305031

Printed in Europe, USA, Canada, Australia, Japan

Cover: Foto ©ninafisch / pixelio.de

More available books at **www.hansebooks.com**

LOST LINKS

IN THE

INDIAN MUTINY.

BY

H. P. MALET,

E.I.C.S.

London:
T. CAUTLEY NEWBY, PUBLISHER,
30, WELBECK STREET, CAVENDISH SQUARE.
1867.

IN LOVE AND DUTY

I DEDICATE THIS LITTLE BOOK

TO MY VENERABLE MOTHER,

THE DOWAGER LADY MALET,

THINKING THAT, IMPERFECT THOUGH IT BE, SHE WILL BE

GLAD TO FIND THAT HER EXAMPLE OF INDUSTRY, OF

MORE THAN HALF-A-CENTURY, HAS

NOT BEEN FORGOTTEN.

SHE WILL RECOGNISE IN THE ESCAPES FROM THE AFGHANS

AND THE TIGER, THE ADVENTURES OF ONE OF HER

SONS, UNDER A FEIGNED NAME, AND

SEE THAT AN EVER-WISE

PROVIDENCE RULETH

OVER ALL.

H. P. MALET.

13th June, 1867.

LOST LINKS IN THE INDIAN MUTINY.

CHAPTER I.

THE MAHOMEDAN CAN ENDURE MUCH.

THERE were no steamers for Hadjis in the days I begin with, though the indefatigable Waghorn had finished his explorations, and had travelled from India to England in a time that was then considered marvellous. The little steamboat "Enterprise" had also made more than one voyage to the Red Sea, in fine weather, and had returned safe.

The Red Sea is never a very cool one; it

was very hot indeed, when the Nacodah (captain) of the grab brig, "Deriah Dowlut," called out to his crew, "Nangar chordo."

The unwieldy, old-fashioned anchor dropped, with a dull splash, in the oily-looking water, and the large coils of the rough kaiar cable disappeared rapidly over the bow.

Several pilgrims stood around, gazing, with varied feelings, on the land of their distant adoration, when my friend Yusuff lost in contemplation, placed a foot within the coils, and was immediately carried overboard.

"Bismillah!" "Khismut!" and several other ready expressions were shouted out, by the devout followers of the prophet, as they leaned over the low bulwarks of the ship, watching, with unchanged countenances, the drowning man.

"He must have been a Sheitan ki Baita!" said one.

"He is gone to Jehannum!" said another.

"We shall have cooler weather now!"

said a third, provoking an audible grin around him, while the poor man, struggling, for a few moments on the surface, sank, with an imploring look beneath the heaving wave.

"Yusuff! Il Allah!" cried out a strong voice, as, at that moment, a man rushed amidst the careless throng; in the next, he had plunged headlong into the sea, just as his friend was rising to the surface; to seize him with one hand, and the now quiet cable with the other, was the work of a moment.

"Wah! wah! God is Great! and Mahomed is His prophet. He will be a Hadji yet!—his sins are washed off!" cried out the astonished spectators.

A boat coming up, Yusuff was taken into it, while his friend and preserver, Hassan, climbing up by the cable, shook out his wet garments on deck, surrounded by the crowd of pilgrims, some expressing their admiration at his courage, some their astonishment at his venturing to interfere with fate, and all gathering together their worldly goods, intent on performing their pilgrimage to Mecca.

"Beled al Harem!" his Holy Land was gained. What did Yusuff care for his wetting!—he had no worldly goods, except a few precious articles on his person; his cotton carpet, at once his bed and his place of prostration in prayer, was fastened round his loins by a white waist cloth. He had no occasion to go on board again, so he staid on shore, prostrating himself in earnest prayer, amidst a Babel of cries for Bakshish to himself, and to the ship load of mixed characters, who were now coming rapidly to the landing place. On rising, he made his way through a dirty, hurrying crowd, to one of the miserable little mosques, several of which were near him. On entering, he drew out one cowrie from his girdle, and gave it to the officiating Moolana, saying,

"May the blessing of God be on the gift of the pauper."

This done, he spread his carpet in a corner, and again prostrated himself in prayer.

It was no love of traffic, no love of wandering, and no mere curiosity, that had induced my friend, Yusuff, to leave his pleasant home, in Jooner—his little garden, with his fig and plantain trees—his small, clear fountain in the centre, which played a multitude of jets on grand occasions—and his pets, the fine murell fish, that sported therein, taking the proffered cockroach from his careful fingers; it was no anxiety to escape from his hard work of paper making—no unhappy home drove him away from his much loved wife, and his little daughter, Ameena, the light-footed, gazelle-eyed houri, the little prattler, who awoke him with a song in the morning, and met him with smiles, as he came home, weary with work, in the evening. He had made this weary journey to offer up his fervent prayers for his poor sickly wife, Fatima, to offer them up with all the devotedness of a true and earnest Mahomedan at the Kaaba, the fountain head of miracles and of mercy, that she might recover her health, and bear him a son; he had dug his well in charity, that the thirsty traveller might drink of its water; he had planted a tree by the roadside, that the heated wanderer might find a little shade; a son alone was wanting to complete his happiness on earth, and to qualify him for the abodes of the blest in Paradise. He expected to find everything grand and clean; his ideas of holiness were associated with cleanliness and splendour; he found it mean and dirty; but he said to himself, "this is only Djedda, I shall be more satisfied at Mecca." He felt weary, his limbs ached, so he determined to rest where he was for the night.

Yusuff awoke, next morning, from troubled dreams—a thick cloud had enveloped him—strange figures struggled within it—blows were given, and blood was flowing—men, women, and children sunk in death—there was lamentation and laughter—his little Ameena struggled in the crowd, and raised her hands in agony; he tried to call her, but she would not come; he tried to catch her, but his limbs failed him. He awoke, cold and trembling—the ague fever was on him; he lay helpless in the miserable corner.

When Hassan left the "Deriah Dowlut," he joined a kafilah, going direct to Mecca—often, during that terrible journey, over fifty odd miles of sandy desert, with nothing but black bread to eat, and bitter water to drink, with his unaccustomed limbs shaken out of their joints by the rough motion of a heavily-laden camel, did he think of what he once called the annoyances of his home in Bhorapoor: What would he not now have given to get them all back again—the heavy taxes, the absence of justice, the extortions of the police, his hard work; and, lastly, the wild fancies of his unruly son, Hoossein—all and each of them far better, and more endurable, than the stifling heat, the choking dust, the horrible stench, the shadeless track over that death-encumbered journey. There were natural and artificial horrors. Hassan was not a delicate individual; yet, he shuddered as he heard the unbridled pilgrims sing their ribald songs, and make their heartless jokes. There was an end, at last, to that dreadful journey—Mecca was reached; and Hassan thanked God and His prophet, with more sincerity than he had ever before done, that he had reached it alive.

"Om el khora" (mother of cities) "Beled el ameyn" (world of believers), rose before him. Where was his own beautiful Taptee river?—where the mosques, the minarets, the palaces, the splendid mausoleums, and the lovely gardens of Bhoraupoor? Hassan's heart sank within him, as he viewed the desolation around—the mean, dirty streets, the filthy people, their unknown language— Al Harem, with its disproportionate colonnades, and its ugly cupolas—the world renowned "Kaaba" (holy of holies) in its centre—all miserable, yet all giving to him, and uncounted numbers, the title for which they had so long and so earnestly panted. His heart failed,—if he could, he would have gone back; but pride forbade him, and he went on, to meet with more and sadder disappointments. His own priests were good and holy men, pure in their conduct, earnest for the benefit of their flocks; here he found the Muftis, Olemas, Mollahs, and Moolanas, all trading, swearing, and drinking. It was no crime for them to seek wealth in the interval of prayer; they were too good, too constant in religious duties, to be under the same rules as the ordinary followers of Mahomed; there was nothing to prevent their relaxation. "Strange!" thought Hassan, as he presented the small offerings he had brought with him, receiving, in return, a careless and hasty benediction.

Hassan was not a devotee, not a saint, even in his own estimation, but a straightforward, strong, courageous man; he had kept the tiger from his herds, the wild boar from his sugar canes. He had an increasing family; the eldest and only son Hoossein, a fine young fellow of fourteen years, was already beyond the father's control; the daughters were many, but some of them dying of cholera, he stayed longer than usual in the Mosque one morning, when the Moolah taking notice of his earnestness advised him to perform a Hadj to pray for his son, and give thanks that he himself had been preserved alive. Hassan was now following this advice; no one performed the ceremonies or offered up his alms and prayers with more apparent sincerity; no one in reality was more disgusted with all he saw. Sad at heart, he went through the prescribed duties, till in the midst of them sickness overtook him, and the strong man lay writhing in the agonies of cholera. His careless companions looked on him as a dying man: death was busy there. Hassan resigned himself to his fate, turned his face from the glare of day, and prayed for his son.

"Hassan!" said a voice by his side.
"Who is it?" was the reply.
"I am Yusuff!"

"I thought," said the dying man, "that you had gone to Paradise; you deserve it when your time comes: I do not. You perform your Hadj from a sense of right; I am only doing as I was bid. There is no Paradise for me."

"God is a better and a more merciful judge than man," replied Yusuff; "we remember our sins when His hands are laid upon us in anger; we repent of them, and make good resolutions for the future."

"God is great, and Mahomed is His prophet; blessed be God!" faintly ejaculated Hassan; "my fate has overtaken me; my limbs are cold; the darkness of futurity falls over my failing sight. Yusuff, my friend, take this packet, it contains a talisman for my son, and a—for—wife."

Hassan's lips quivered as he spoke, his lower jaw fell, his glazed eyes opened wide, a slight convulsion passed over him, the man was dead.

Yusuff buried his companion, and having finished the prescribed ceremonies—all the quicker on account of his poverty, his single-mindedness, and his universal charity, which, perceiving none of the objectionable outward inconveniences of Mecca, knew it only as the birth-place of him on whom all his faith and hope was placed—prepared to depart He joined a party going to Mocha, and having waited for some time in the vain hope of finding a vessel sailing to India, he at last followed the example of his neigbours, and spread his carpet on the deck of a Persian dhow.

The winds were fair down the Red Sea, through the straits of Babel Mandeb, and for a short distance beyond ; then the horrors of that terrible voyage commenced; the atmosphere was burning hot; the glassy sea heaved with an idle, melancholy swell ; the large sail hung heavily, or flapped, as the boat rolled, with a loud, monotonous sound; the sun burnt them by day, and the heavy dew wetted them by night. There was no escape, no place to rest in, no world for those weary pilgrims, but the dirty deck or the oily sea. Everything seemed to combine against them, and as if the elements were not sufficient, man added his petty tyranny for the occasion, and the vermin made their meals on the enfeebled Pilgrims; they were ordered about as brute beasts, kicked and cuffed by that cruel crew; they could get no redress, they were too weak—too miserable—to help themselves; their water was offensive to drink, their food was loathsome to eat; one after another the poor men died. Their effects were seized by the sailors, who looked over the side of their ship, and laughed as they watched the ravenous sharks fighting for their ghastly prey.

Luckily for the few survivors, they were unexpectedly relieved from their misery; a light breeze sprung up, a sail was seen, the captain steered so as to speak with the stranger; he did not know where he was, and found that the currents had carried him far out of his course. The buggalow "Bhow Persaud" was bound from the Persian Gulf to Bombay with a cargo of horses; the Nacoxdah consented to take Yusuff and two others, who joyfully accepted the change, not forgetting to offer up their prayers for those they left behind them, Yusuff remarking that that awful ship required some special assistance from Providence.

Gaily sailed the "Bhow Persaud;" the Nacodah was a skilful mariner, his crew were brave seamen, the enormous lateen sail was well handled, and in a few days the lighthouse of Bombay was seen. The sea breeze blew fresh and fair, the islands of Henry Kenry were passed; the pent up horses neighed loudly as they passed, and in a few minutes the vessel reached the Musjid Bunder. Yusuff was very thankful to see it again; he went on shore, and walked quickly to the house of a friend.

After a week's rest, Yusuff felt equal to the long journey before him. At the time I allude to, the Concan, through which his route lay, was infested by robbers; the Hadji, as he was now commonly called, was advised to take a guard.

"I have nothing to lose but my poverty," said he. "Mecca has got even the skin of my teeth."

So he started; it was a laborious and a weary march, as day by day he trudged along that dusty road. He longed to climb to the top of those blue mountains, which stretched their wall-like line before him. Glad was he when one evening he reached their base, and stepped off the road to perform his ablutions in a clear stream that flowed beside it, hoping, in an hour or two, to find a resting place for the night in the pure night air of the summit. While he was in the water, he heard the sound of dry leaves crackling; he looked up, and on the high bank of the river, some twenty yards above him, a large tiger was stealthily creeping along. Yusuff held his breath, and remained motionless; on a sudden the beast stood still with ears erect; the sound of human voices came down the vale; the wild animal vanished, and Yusuff breathed again. While he was dressing, he became aware that armed men were round him; they asked him who he was, and what he was doing there.

"I am a poor Hadji," he replied, "on my way home."

"Just the man for us; we require a little piety amongst us; so come along on a new Hadj with Ragogee Bangria. You must fight for him, and avenge the poor on their oppressors."

"I fight?" said Yusuff, with horror. "I come with you? impossible! Look here," he said, holding up his lacerated feet, and extending his emaciated arms; "your battles would fare badly with such miserable help as mine."

His excuse was of no avail; he was forced to go on and on, up through bye paths, along the rugged mountain side, in the beds where torrents once had run; along the edge of precipices, and through dark ravines, they travelled, in silence, in Indian file; not a word was spoken; a careless footstep, or the cracking of a dead stick beneath the foot, were the only sounds heard in that stilly march. Yusuff, weary ere he started, was now worn out with fatigue; often was he tempted to fall down and submit to the fate which was promised him; when just as he felt that it was utterly impossible for him to go further, the gang stopped on the edge of a deep ravine; a whispered conversation ensued; clothes were laid aside, and he was given to understand that his duty was to stop and guard them.

He was left sitting on a black rock, in the black night. He was no coward, yet a feeling of dread and trouble crept over him; it completely absorbed him, so that he forgot his fatigue, his pain, and even his desire to escape. After a time an irresistible impulse to see what was going on, took possession of him; he followed a small path, guided by a distant flickering light, and the sound of many voices.

CHAPTER II.

HOW THE NATIVES OF INDIA EAT UP ONE ANOTHER.

To enable my readers to comprehend the position in which the Hadji is now placed, it is necessary to go back for many years to shew that the evil I wish to delineate is neither of late origin nor of accidental birth, but that it pervades Indian society as a thing of course; that forcible rapacity, as a combination of ignorance and injured strength, becomes at once an object of legal persecution, while secret rapacity, the child of cunning education, is too often left to the natural avenger, and though more deeply injuring the community in which it exists, it frequently escapes with complete immunity from the law.

A type of the latter came under my observation in the person of one Dundedass, born in a small village of Rajpootana, where his father kept a shop, a credit and debit account with his poor neighbours, and held a small quantity of land in mortgage from an unfortunate ryot, who had expended more than he could ever repay on the marriage of his son.

The naked little cherub would sit for hours together watching his respected parent making up his accounts from the sand-covered board, and transferring them to his books; he shared the old man's pleasure when a satisfactory bill was fabricated; he was quite conversant with various weights and measures, as well as with the extra notch for the balance of the scales.

Left alone in the shop one day, a poor woman

offered a golden trinket for sale. It had been brought before. Dundedass recollected it, and the value his father had placed on it; the youngster declared it had lost weight; the woman's necessities received the smaller sum, but the original value was taken from the box, and entered on the board, the difference being carefully concealed.

The apparent innocence, the aptitude, and success in dealing of the child, soon gave much of the shop business to him. Their trade was increasing till a bit of rascality brought the old man under the notice of the authorities.

Amongst other victims of his rapacity was a fair Nautch girl. He sued Ailee, on what represented her own bond, for her house and for money. Ailee denied the debt, declaring that the whole bond had been altered, and that though she had given one for a certain sum of money, this was not the same. As she had frequently amused the native judge with dance and song, he was inclined to listen to her tale, so, contrary to the suggestions of his clerk, who well knew the value of old Dundedass, messengers were sent to bring all the shop books and records for inspection.

This was a job gladly undertaken, as many small pickings were expected.

Young Dundedass was found sitting in the shop; he at once volunteered to shew every thing: books were brought out, loose papers shewn, pots and pans emptied of their miscellaneous contents, and he declared that no place remained unsearched. The messengers were not quite satisfied; they ransacked a little more, and in a dusty nook discovered the boy's secret treasures. His little bits of jewellery, fragments of gold and silver, stray original accounts, including the very one sought for (supposed by the father to be all safe), with many other trifles, all very sweet, because stolen, were swept away in the capacious kumer bunds of the judge's retainers, who carefully delivered to their superior all the papers, books and money, retaining the trifles not likely to be entered on the records.

Dundedass was horror struck to see papers produced which he thought were gone, now carefully arranged and put together. He cursed the acquisitive genius of his son, which consigned him to prison, and his goods to confiscation.

Ailee looked beautiful, and the judge was glad that he had been of service to her.

Dundedass, finding himself thus early in life on his own resources, his instinct did not fail him; he coaxed some of his father's creditors to give him a little money for the poor old man's immediate necessities; then slinging his brazen lota over his shoulders, he started on his worldly career. He had no letters of introduction, but his handsome features, his youth, his writing, and his figures, procured for some years a fluctuating income. Travelling westward, he at last reached a village, near the confines of the Deccan, named "Wary Warra;" as there was no shopkeeper there, and plenty of poor people in the village, and in the surrounding mountains, who frequently required assistance, he made up his mind to stay there.

Dundedass soon drove a thriving trade amongst the ignorant cultivators of the plains, and the Cooley tribes of the western Ghauts; his success procured him a beautiful young bride from the neigbouring city of Nassick, and his wife's wealthy brother, Luckmedass, joined him in his trade; the country around was rich and fertile, the inhabitants indigent, ignorant, and careless; our Wanees made from seventy-five to two hundred per cent.; lands, cattle, and human beings fell in on mortgage.

Prosperity did not improve Dundedass; some said that Luckmedass was the worst of the two, but they only acted on the universal fashion, and got all they could; it was indifferent to them how they got it, provided they did not infringe the laws. Dundedass had studied these carefully; as he read them he had chuckled to himself, he had laughed aloud. "Aye!" he said, one day, "stamp duties to pay? so much per cent. The heavier

I make my bills the less chance of these poor people contesting them!" Long impunity made them rash; they took too great an advantage of a bad season, their well filled granaries realised thousands of rupees, but brought down a reckoning upon which they had not calculated.

There are tribes of men living amidst the fastnesses and the jungles of western India, who subsist on natural productions of the soil and the chase, whose cultivation is of the rudest kind, and whose wants are easily satisfied, yet with whom there are periodical discontents. It is quite possible this may be their normal condition: fear may keep them quiet, or a fearless leader may bring them into notice.

There was a solitary hut high up on the hills, overlooking the northern Concan; at its door sat a young woman, nursing a male child. Luximun Jemindar, of the Tanna Police, passing by, remarked to her that he had hung the father, and would, in all probability, hang the son.

"You hang him?" retorted the enraged woman, with the volubility of her race. "You shall never live to do so. If I do not succeed in killing you myself, I will leave the duty as a legacy to this infant. You have made him fatherless, and me a widow; even now he sucks in revenge; it shall be the only lesson I shall teach him; go!"

Eighteen years had passed away; the threat was forgotten, the woman was dead, and Luximun was scouring the jungles for some petty thieves; the day was breaking over the high hills above him, but the deep valley was still in darkness. The policemen left their Jemadar in a hut to go down to the trickling rill, which ran a few yards below them. Luximun stood in the doorway—a fine old fellow, grey headed, and white whiskered. He was dressed in his uniform, with a pair of beautiful pistols in his waistband, which had been presented to him by government for his activity and good conduct against the predatory tribes.

"I am Ragogee Bangria!" said a light figure, suddenly standing before him. "You hung my father and insulted my mother! Die!"

Luximun had drawn a pistol, but it was too late: he was cut down in silence. His head was sent as a present to the magistrate of Tanna.

Ragogee Bangria, the descendant of a long line of Cooley Naigues, robbers and outlaws of many generations, thus began his short career as an avenger. The poor man was his friend, the rich money-lender his enemy. The valleys below the mountains, the plains above, were visited by the gang. Rajogee was here, there, and everywhere; the rapidity and the distances of his visitations were most extraordinary. The police of two districts were foiled, and several of them killed; military aid was called out, high rewards were offered for his capture, but Ragogee was, on the night I allude to, at Wary Warra.

Yusuff, as I said before, forgetting pain and fatigue, crept stealthily along a small path till he approached the scene of violence. By the flickering light of many torches he saw two tall men standing with bound hands before Ragogee. He saw a sum of money brought and counted; it was not sufficient,— more was demanded; it was not forthcoming.

"Cut off their noses!" cried the young leader.

It was done. The money was still refused.

"Bring some cotton!" ordered Ragogee.

It was brought. It was bound over the limbs of the prisoners, and oil was then poured over it. A demand was again made for more money. Dundedass offered a valuable jewel, and told them where to find it; it was not there.

"Tie them to the stake!"

They were tied to the stake that stood in the midst of their own threshing floor—that stake around which bullocks, not their own, had so often trod out the grain, which they had neither sown nor reaped. Dry fuel was heaped around them.

"Light the fire!" cried the leader.

Dundedass and Luckmedass prayed for their lives, and they would give all they had.

"You are rogues!" cried Ragogee. "Where is the jewel?"

The straw began to blaze. A dreadful scream was heard, and the young, beautiful wife, tearing herself away from the ruthless hands of her persecutors, rushed with torn garments and dishevelled hair, through the rising flames, and fell motionless on the feet of Dundedass.

A streak of light shot up in the eastern sky, and a gleam of pity entered the hearts of the avengers. The fire was quickly pulled away. Ragogee and his gang disappeared—Yusuff never knew how. So intent was he on the miserable group before him, that he remained spell-bound and motionless, leaning on a broken wall.

The day began to grow, voices were heard approaching. Our friend Yusuff was seized with a cry of "Here is one of them!"

"Tie him up!" cried out the police officer, for it was the Nassick police that had come.

The miserable group were still around the stake; the flickering light from the still burning beams of the house threw a quivering glimmer over a scene too sad for the sun to rise upon. Dundedass and Luckmedass, faint with loss of blood, were untied and attended to; the beautiful and innocent Gungee was picked up, a scorched and lifeless corpse.

Yusuff was taken before the magistrates of the district, to whom he told the details of his unsought adventure, his miserable condition; and his name, which was known at Nassick, vouched for his truth, and he was released.

A few years after this Ragogee Bangria's gang was broken up; he, after a long concealment, was betrayed to an active police officer, and being caught in the performance of the religious duties of a good Hindoo at the celebrated temple of Punderpoor, in due course of time was hung.

Dundedass and Luckmedass, the roots of the evil, had their features rectified as neatly as possible, and may, even as I write, be again occupied in eating up their neighbours.

CHAPTER III.

THE MAN TO RULE.

Yusuff found at Nassick Mahomedans whom he knew, and learning from them that his wife and little daughter Ameena had gone to Dowlutabad with his brother Yacoob, under whose care they had been left, and as this was a long journey, he decided on remaining where he was till he felt better able to travel.

It so happened that during his stay the annual Jatrah of Trimbuck took place; this was a Hindoo affair; but his friends wishing to see it, and feeling quite secure in their orthodoxy by the presence of a veritable Hadji, persuaded our traveller to go with them, though he had some misgivings lest his example should be a snare and a delusion to others. So they made up a pleasant party in vehicles, drawn by bullocks, and visited the curious and sacred old city of Trimbuck.

Situated in a country remarkable for its beautiful scenery, the town, with its strange, fantastic, yet elegant fanes, stands at the foot of a mountain, on the summit of which is the nearly inaccessible fort of Trimbuck, the only approach to which is by climbing up a perpendicular cliff; in this steps have been cut, narrow and far apart, each step having a niche cut on it, for the more secure hold of the adventurous climber.

This was the first religious assembly that Yusuff had seen since Mecca; he was struck with the devotion of the Hindoos, the pious solemnity of their rites, the severity of their penances, and the strictness with which they performed their vows, even to their own detriment. He saw the sacred waters of the Young Godavery flowing from the mouth of the sculptured cow high up on the mountain's side; he traced the silver stream in its wooded banks down the beautiful vale, till his eye rested on the shady groves of Gungapoor, where he and his friends stopped on their return.

Gungapoor (city of the Gunga) is one of those charming spots which Hindoo religion loves to select as the threshold of the unknown world—the air is cool, water plentiful, foliage abundant, and the rugged hills at no great distance; here the loving friends of the Brahmin widows loved to usher them, by the rites of suttee, into the arms of their departed husbands; here the living and dead were buried together; and here the suttee temples still shew in their neatness, their magnificence, or their purity, the mournful feelings of the inheriting relations.

Eastern rivers, near the places of incremation, are generally sacred; their pools are full of fish, the vicinity also produces plenty, and the villages around provide fishermen. The Mussulman is naturally addicted to the amusement. On the day in question they had their long lines in their knmer bunds; a bit of paste was the bait, and the Hadji, standing on the bank, was much amused at his friends' pulling out the scaly prizes from the rocky pools, where the torrents had excavated deep holes, where the waters eddied and foamed, and where the big fish had found a place to dwell in. As the party approached the temples they stopped their sport, wound up their lines, and went home; ill would it have fared with them if they had polluted one drop of the sacred pool.

Not many years ago the writer of this tale was on a visit to the magistrate of the district; a fishing excursion was proposed, rods and tackle prepared, and in the morning we rode off to the river side. Our intention had got abroad; the old Patell (head of the village) met us, and as he had heard of our intentions hoped we would graciously accept the present he had prepared for us, pointing, as he spoke, to a cart load of silver beauties, which lay kicking under a mango tree. Our disgust may be imagined, but the intended civility was accepted. We did not abuse our considerate friend till out of hearing. On another occasion the writer was fishing on the verge of the sacred precincts, when a strong party of angry Brahmins, intent on turning him off, came up, and demanded that he should not kill fish; he immediately complied, wound up his line, and walked with his friends to the temple steps. Sitting down he opened his small morocco leather case of materials, and made a fresh fly; the ferocious Brahmins watching the operation intently. When it was finished he offered them his rod, and begged they would try to catch a fish; they did so, very much to the amusement of the spectators, and much to their own astonishment at their awkwardness. When tired with their own futile attempts they asked him if that little bit of green wool and bunch of feathers really would catch a fish? Taking the old Chevallier in hand, and giving a very slight crack with the fly over their heads, it fell light as a feather on a curl of the stream beside a rock; there was an almost imperceptible whirl, but the line tightened; then came a heavy plunge, a long dash down the rapid, a few struggles in the pool below, and a five pound Rhoo lay kicking before them. "Do not kill it on the temple steps," they said. "May he be killed anywhere?" was the reply. "As you please!" The writer walked into the stream, and seeing the unfeigned horror expressed in some of the faces before him, he unhooked the fish and let him go. The holiest of holies were delighted. How easy it is to rule such people!

To return to my story. Yusuff wandered along this beautiful river. He was told that its waters were too holy for agricultural or ordinary purposes; he scarcely believed this, though he did feel much refreshed by a wash in it.

The Hadji soon found himself getting strong and hearty in his native air, so bidding adieu to his friends he continued his journey, in a few days reaching a place of some note, Mhijee. He had timed his journey with the intention of witnessing the great fair, which, once a year, is held in this small village. At the distance of some miles he overtook, or was passed by many people flocking to the same place. The earth was dry and dusty, and over the fair hung the dim canopy, shutting out the glare of the sun, nearly choking the assembled multitudes.

The stalls, shops, or open sheds, were full of costly and useful articles, from all parts of the world. England and America were represented by their cotton fabrics; there were shawls from France, and watches from Geneva; China had sent her ivory, feather punkahs, and her coffee cups; there were bales of rich fabrics from Cashmere; tissues and pictures from Delhi; curiosities in gold and silver from Madras; guns and swords from Persia; and hanging out in long festoons were the light and elegant muslins of Dacca. The streets were full of divers nations and languages, strange in character, curious in costume.

In the bed of the river, now nearly dry, two elephants were goaded into a slow race to exhibit their unwieldy speed; many pairs of bullocks, warranted to draw any weight, were endeavouring to pull laden carts through the impassable sand, suffering excruciating twists of their unfortunate tails, which, in the drivers' opinion, were only made to be twisted; there were young horses curvetting, prancing, galloping, and stopping dead under the control of the Mahratta bit; there was a tame royal tiger, walking about behind its master, ready to eat up any goat that was given to it, and no other. There were many other curiosities in the animal line, which did not attract much of Yusuff's attention; he looked at, and was sorry for a miserable faqueer, who had stood so long on one leg, that the other was shrunk up into a useless limb of skin and bone. Close behind him stood a ghastly man, covered with ashes; his offending hand clasped tightly together for so long a time, that his finger nails had grown through, and out at the back. A little farther on, a pair of dirty black feet stuck up in the air, whilst all the rest of the Hindoo owner was buried in the ground, expiating some unheard of sin, and expecting alms for his endurance.

On the high bank of the river, so that every one could see the performance, a poor deluded victim was swinging round in the air, suspended by an iron hook, passed through the muscles of his back, fastened to a horizontal pole, balanced on an upright one by heavy weights at the other end, with a string attached, so that the officiating priest might give an extra jerk now and then, when he thought any passers by would be induced to give him an extra piece for the agony endured.

Yusuff wondered at all this; his own vows rose in troubled memories before him. Few, very few Hadjis would do this. "We endure a good deal, no doubt, but we forget our sorrows; these men can never forget theirs."

Yusuff wandered observingly amidst the crowd; he wondered how all the concourse were gathered together in this out-of-the-way corner. He was told it was an old fashion; that it had been in disuse for some years during the times of the Pindarees and the Bheels; that since General Wellesley Sahib had conquered the Mahrattas, and Outram Sahib had quieted the Bheels, the magistrate himself, or one of his assistants, yearly encamped on the spot to preserve order; that the trouble taken by the authorities in securing safety to life and property, encouraged traders to assemble.

"Look there," said a man, to whom he was speaking, pointing to a long line of white tents; "there is the magistrate's camp; any offender is taken there at once, and no one complains without his meeting with immediate attention."

The attractions of Mhijee ended, Yusuff pursued his journey, and soon saw the range of hills, on the top of which he hoped to be re-united to his family. As the evening closed in, he climbed the ascent to Rosa; and in one of the tombs he found Fatima, his wife, and Ameena, his daughter, with the children of his brother Yacoob.

An East Indian Mahomedan girl, of ten years old, is sometimes a charming picture. Yusuff gazed on such an one, while little Ameena trimmed the wicks of the lamp, which ever shed its light on the tomb of the renowned dervish. Her skin was a light olive brown, soft and velvety, a darker shade suffusing the cheek occasionally. This cheek was round, and full to perfection; her little chin was dimpled and movable, the lips seldom seemed quite to close—or, if they did meet, the ivory teeth glittered through the rosy joining. The nose was the most imperfect feature, but if inclination cavilled at it, admiration again resumed its sway in the black and lustrous eyes, which, full of soft expression, gazed with love on the weather-worn face of her father, as he recountered his adventures to the little circle.

Yusuff forgot all his troubles in this hallowed dwelling; to his spirit the spot was sacred. The mausoleums held the remains of the great departed, the trees around had been planted so as to give perpetual verdure, and a grateful shade. But not alone on the hill top was he happy; there were delights and wonders on the abrupt mountain sides. It was a pleasure to all the circle to roam through the caves of Ellora. There was the elaborate cave temple of Khylass; there were also many others completed, and many the finishing of which had been prevented by one of those extraordinary accidents which will sometimes happen, even to so all foreseeing a divinity as Juggernath.

There, in front of the mighty cave, he sits with his never-failing slaves, Jay and Bigel, waiting on him, surveying his labours with infinite satisfaction. His obsequious attendants, Sud and Bud, stand attentive at the door of the Temple, ready to act as grooms of the chamber, when Juggernath shall please to walk; but time was lost in contemplating the never failing wonders, and the extraordinary works of Bishkurna (World Creator) head carpenter to the ruler Ramchindur, who, with wise forethought and care to prevent interruption to these works, as well as to the extraordinary excavations then in progress for the great hill fortress of Deoghur, now Dowbutabad—had bespoken a night of six months' duration, and the whole of the works were in a satisfactory condition; when a wild young jungle cock, forgetting the injunction to silence which he had received, jumped up on a bough of a tree, flapped his wings three times, and crowed as loud as he could.

Of course the morning awoke with its every-day occupations; and all the workmen gathered together from great distances with much labour, went away to their usual avocations. Much work was left undone, but Juggernath remains, contemplating the scene; there he still sits, as he sat when this occurred, all the same, barring natural decay, as the excavations and temples were then unfortunately left.

Let us take a peep at the objects of the god's inspection. There are wonderful cave temples all around the hill side; the most beautiful is Khylass. The outer area is a square of one hundred and eight feet; the inner one measures two hundred and forty-seven, by one hundred and fifty feet. In the midst of this stands the sacred shrine, not built with mortar, but hewn from the hard black rock of the mountain side; its architecture and sculpture displaying science, ingenuity, patience and perseverance, prompting our admiration of the skill of a people who produced such wonderful results.

The gateway, rich in battlements, bastions, and turrets, welcomes fresh arrivals with cherubs and seraphs smiling of face, joyous in attitude. Here are rooms for those who hang about the portals, like the poor ghosts who wandered by the shores of the Styx, unable to pay the cost of the ferry. Above is the orchestra for dulcimer and sackbut; here blew out the horn to the new moon, and all kinds of music ushered the blessed into the sacred realms, where the light of Heaven, descending through the excavated shaft, glimmers dimly and scantily on its grand and everlasting blackness. Its pillars, turrets, walls, caves, and roof, inside and outside, are carved full of grotesque shapes of mythical figures, divine, human, and animal, of varied, strange, yet elegant arrangement. There is an upper and lower paradise, there are narrow paths for the careless to miss, there are bridges for the rash to fall over, there are horrid animals and serpents to frighten the timid, while temptations of divers forms, in strong relief, are festooned around to attract the uncertain, and to confirm the steadfast.

Gods and goddesses of eastern prowess are here in peace and quietness; attendants, favourites, and victims are all delineated in the unfeeling stone, all telling their marvellous tales to a now nearly satisfied credulity. Paradise is well filled; there is scarcely room for more without inconvenient crowding. Time has corroded much, the curiosity and acquisitiveness of man has destroyed more, but enough remains to satisfy the most anxious—to weary the most patient inspector.

Many have inspected these works of art with greater results than the god Juggernath. They have brought away with them pictures, measurements, and full descriptions, recondite and profuse, which are supposed to be somewhere amidst the dusty archives of the Indian office, to which I take the liberty of referring any one in whom I may succeed in stirring up the faintest interest towards these wonders of India.

Our Hadji would have gladly remained in the neighbourhood of the sacred places of Bramah and Budda. His was a pleasant resting place in the mausoleums of dervishes; and great men, whose names and tombs had lasted hundred of years. More than one Oriental dynasty was commemorated on this spot, which alone retained the impression; and as Yusuff looked on the thick jungle, the deserted villages, and the broken roads, he almost dreaded to start again on a journey; but the dying message of his friend, Hassan, had to be delivered — the son, Hoosscin, had to be discovered.

. Yusuff had no dread of any visitation from Providence. Ever since he was a boy, he had heard of the Bheels of Khandesh, as robbers and murderers. The vision still haunted him, and rose up vividly, as the day of his departure approached. His friends assured him that the roads were safe, that all the Bheels in the country through which his road ran were now industrious and peaceful people; that they lived in huts, instead of on the hill-side, and would never rob or murder again. They told him how a single young Englishman had effected the change; how he had held a talk with the old, and collected the young men into an army; that he had hunted with them on the hill-tops, and had visited their mountain fortresses; and how the old Bheel Naiques, whose hands had been against every man, had visited Outram Saheb Bahadoor, in his grand house, at Durungaum. Such a house had never been seen by them—large and grand, with lofty rooms and cool verandahs, with great pictures and splendid trophies of the chase; they loved to look on the skins of the lion and the tiger—to handle the long tusk of the boar, the claw of the bear, the horn

D

of the bison; they looked around that reception room, and found no wild animal, within their knowledge, unrepresented. Then there were the implements of the chase, such as they had never seen or dreamed of—everything around attracted their respect, an acquaintance with the man produced a veneration—such a man had never been heard of. There could be no use in opposing one who would as soon face the tiger as the hare—whose horse could catch the buffalo—who would beard the bear in his den—who could, in fact, do everything.

On these representations Yusuff started. He met with no adventures; but where anarchy and ruin had been, he found the people contented, happy, and recovering their prosperity. The encroaching jungles were reduced, cultivation increased; and the chaos, which had existed only a few short years before, was gone.

"Who has done it all?" was the repeated enquiry of the Hadji.

The only reply he received was, "It is all done by James Outram Saheb Bahadoor."

CHAPTER IV.

HOOSSEIN—BEN HASSAN, AND HIS MOTTO.

CHOTEE MA sat by her house-door, looking out on the lovely Taptee river. She was a lone woman now—her husband far away, her young son seldom with her. There was a shade over her existence, like that which now, at eventide, fell on the mirror-like surface of the stream before her; her hopes had flitted away like the shadows of the lofty minarets and gilded cupolas—like those of the strong towers of the palaces of kings. They would not stay, but lengthened and spread; every moment they climbed the further banks of the river, sprung over the abrupt and tangled steeps beyond, enveloped the wide forests, then crept up the distant hills, till all was wrapped in the hazy purple of an eastern sunset, except the pinnacle of a distant mountain; her eyes were fixed on this one light spot of the charming landscape—her hopes had dwindled to a smaller point—her thoughts were as slow and quiet as the summer river at her feet, and she heard not the footsteps of the man who now stood before her.

Yusuff quietly announced himself, and in a few words told his tale. The darkness of night enveloped her, as it did the scene but just now before her. There was no more light for her, Hassan could not come back, and Hoossein would not remain at home. She sat, for a time, helpless in her sorrow; then thoughts of hospitality crept over her; she lighted her oil vase, she was preparing her evening meal, when a light step entered the room.

Yusuff looked up; a brilliant youth of some fifteen summers stood before them, faultless of feature, daring of carriage, ardent in expression.

"Like his father, the Hadji," said Yusuff, as he undid a girdle from his waist.

"My talisman!" exclaimed Chotee Ma, as a small silver box was exposed to view. "Your father is dead, Hoossein; no one could have got this while he was alive." She took it from Yusuff's hand, and, opening a clasp, said, 'See here, my son; here is your genealogy,—for one hundred and seventy generations the name has remained unchanged. Your family have reckoned kings and princes among them. Your ancestors have been the greatest in the land, and your progenitor was our Holy Prophet, blessed be his name! And here, my Seyud son, is your nativity, cast while yet you were, but one hour old. On this are inscribed the signs of your future existence."

"Let me see it," said Hoossein, seizing the little roll of paper rather roughly. "Ah!" he cried, "here they are—an antelope, a roomal, a swallow, a tortoise, a serpent; then there are great flames and smoke, human figures and raging tigers, a woman with dishevelled hair, a tree with only one bough, and a scroll at the bottom, with

'WHAT THOU DOEST, DO.'

"Of course I shall," laughingly remarked the young man.

"Why do you laugh?" said his mother. "Your father is dead."

"Yes, I know it," he replied. "I saw it in a dream. My father died in a miserable, dirty hole—insects and lizards crawling about, and only this old friend attending his first steps towards Paradise. I knew he would come and bring the amulet. How I have longed to see it; and now it has come, I can make nothing of it. I thank you, friend of my father, for bringing it safe, through all the troubles you have seen on your journey. I have watched you often, and I feared that you would never come."

"But you never said anything about it," meekly observed his mother.

"If I told you all I saw in my dreams, mother, you would not own me for your son, or believe that I am human. I hold long converse with Shitan, and walk through the furnaces of Jehannum. I am familiar with unknown monsters, and talk with the spirits of those who have left us. There are but few of my friends in Paradise, but many who have got into difficulties on the way. Mother, can we do nothing for my father?— he is still knocking at the outer gate, and no one comes to open it."

Yusuff here observed that flippant conversation was neither pleasant to others or becoming to himself.

"I was never more serious," replied the young man. "I have never ceased to dream of these things since I saw the strange monsters in the caves of Ellora, when I was betrothed to Ameena. I must now cease dreaming, and act for myself. As soon as the funeral rites are performed, I start on my career of life. The fates have been consulted, and I am to enter the service of a Feringhee."

"When your father's affairs are settled you can go," said Chotee Ma. "There are his fields and his houses."

"Keep them yourself, mother," said Hoossein, "and what you do not want, give to the Moollah, it will alleviate my father's anxiety, and be a prepayment of prayers for his son; he will require plenty if he fulfils his destiny."

Nothing more was said; the obsequies were duly performed, and in a few days Hoossein became a servant in the house of an English military officer.

No one was more assiduous in his duties than Hoossein ; he found time to learn the English language, he became a great favourite in the establishment; there was no one so obliging, or so attentive to the commands of the Mem Saheb, or so good natured to the little children, with whom, when duty permitted, he would play for hours. This happy time was soon over. Before two years expired an agent of the King of Delhi took notice of him, and Hoossein was hired as one of the running footmen to the Mirror of Justice, the King of the Universe.

"I am an antelope," thought the young man, as dressed in a robe of pure white, with red kumer bund, he, with several others, ran in procession before the Admiration of the World, and when neither duty nor pleasure induced his Majesty to leave the seraglio, these young men lounged about the palace chatting together, and looking at the forbidden lattices.

Hoossein at this time never doubted but

that the shaking, bejewelled old man was indeed the greatest king of the world. His palace was a large one, his zenana was a full one ; his pomp, his magnificence could never be equalled. Ambition is prone to copy what it sees succeed, so Hoossein hung the skirts of his faith on the decrepid fabric of indulgence.

It was an idle state of existence, and the young men caused much anxiety in the heart of the superintendent of the seraglio.

The eunuch, Sooba, was a very useful guardian, and right honestly did he serve his master; but as to the rest of creation, he considered it only as subservient to one great end —his Majesty's will and pleasure. It was his duty to minister to these, and therefore it was no consequence to him whether he dealt with the living or the dead; it was thought that he had a strong leaning to the latter, particularly if his own hand had been instrumental in the transfer. It was supposed advisable to conciliate Sooba by presents, if life was valued. Young men occasionally disappeared no one knew how, and it was whispered that faces had vanished from the lattices like meteors from the heavens. Sooba's hand was always on his dagger, his eye was full of suspicion, and his diabolical countenance did not belie him; the king knew his value, and reposed full confidence in him.

Sooba, however, could not be every where at once, so, as his haunts and habits were well known, it did not require much ingenuity to cast dust in his eyes. The ladies understood this art remarkably well, and though they fully comprehended the risk they ran, yet they ventured to try, and managed to succeed in attracting the attention of the new Juwan. Immunity begat carelessness, and as Hoossein was one day talking to the magnificent and imperious Tara, he was detected by Sooba himself. The guardian said nothing, but as he passed, Hoossein caught the glance of that villanous eye, and feeling that he was in danger, stood upon his guard. All that night, and for several nights, Hoossein was aware of certain watches put over him; he could not sleep, for he knew the fate that would overtake him; he found that his food was tampered with—he left it untouched; he endeavoured to get out of the palace, but on one excuse or another he was prevented. There seemed to be no escape; he might keep off the danger for a time, but he was almost wearied out, and began to look upon death as a relief from his trouble. While drawing this conclusion, nature was giving way, and he almost slept. He started; something touched his face.

"Silence! Follow me!" was said in a whisper close to his ear.

Hoossein arose, and stepping lightly followed a female form, carrying a dim light, through several open doors, all of which were carefully locked after them.

"I can get you no farther," said his guide. "Here are clothes for you," and before he could think about it he was enveloped in female garb, with a thick veil over his face.

It was in the early grey of the morning that Sooba came to look after the guards he had placed to destroy Hoossein if an opportunity occurred of doing it quietly. They were asleep, and his intended victim gone. He looked out of the open lattice on to a descent of seventy feet; it was too dark to see plainly, but it struck him that something like the form of a man lay below.

"If," thought he, "the young man is there, he will be devoured in an hour by pigs and dogs."

Then he thought he must have gone that way, for if he had succeeded in escaping the special watches, he could not have gone past the regular guards of the palace without being seen.

There was indeed a concealed door leading to the zenana, a door which he had himself used at midnight, when he found Hoossein on the watch, but the key was on his girdle ; he never thought of the master key, or if he did it was safe in the care of Zeenaut Mahal

Begum, the favourite lady of the harem, but she was the dear friend of Tara. In fact, the guardian was puzzled, and he did not dare to make any stir in the matter, for fear of attracting that attention from his Majesty which would have closed his own career.

Hoossein kept no record of the days he passed in concealment; he knew that there was a perpetual alarm, and fear of detection, possibly increased and exaggerated by the women, who, not understanding the whole truth, were yet aware that there was a secret in the harem. There was much uneasiness attending this sort of existence, with a pretty clear idea how it would end if detected, so that he felt much relieved when he was requested to follow two female figures through the long arcades of the garden. They led the way through a narrow low door, and as he passed a female voice whispered in his ear to get into the bullock gharee he would find outside, to do as he was told to do, and in the morning he would find friends.

Hoossein gladly obeyed these instructions. The cart was a covered one, as if it contained women. He heard the pass-word given, at the gate, and some jokes that went on between his driver and the guard; after a time he looked out, and was aware that the road ran through many ruins of mosques, temples, and tombs of generations long passed away. In about two hours the driver stopped, and told Hoossein to get out and conceal himself in one of the court yards of a mosque beside them—that in the morning some one would come and tell him what to do.

Hoossein hesitated for a moment before stepping into the dark, dismal, solitary building before him, but he was very weary—he had not slept for many nights, so in he went, almost careless of consequences, and sought a quiet corner amidst the mass of lofty columns which rose before him in the dim light of the midnight rising moon; at last he crept into one of the domed corners of the quadrangle, in the midst of which stood the iron pillar of Feroze Shah. Here Hoossein took off his female dress, and rolling it into a pillow, soon fell fast asleep.

The sun was shining into the great square of Khootab Mina, when Hoossein was awoke by the sound of many voices and much laughter.

"He is in the Jumna," said one.

"The tortoises will like him!" said another.

"Perhaps he is buried in the garden," was remarked.

"Good for the custard apples," was rejoined.

"Yes; arsenic will improve their flavour," hinted another of these light hearted gentry.

"He is here," said a tall, black bearded man, whom Hoossein had seen before, and who accosted him as Seyud Hoossein Saheb.

In a corner not far off two or three men were busy preparing breakfast; there were sundry little fires with iron plates over them, resting on the corners of rough stones. On these the everlasting roti was preparing; rice was boiling in a large earthen pot; one man was busy skewering up, on bits of reed, kabobs composed of meat, onions, and green ginger; another was mixing, on a flat stone, a quantity of brown material—by him called masallah, by us curry; and soon the whole party sat amidst the wondrous relics of greater days to make their breakfast in the midst of religious emblems of a more devout race. Mussulman and Hindoo, Brama and Bud, had each selected that place for their buildings. Gods and men, monkeys and animals of varied kind, in studied sculpture, looked down with their stony eyes on the equally hard hearts of this Thug fraternity.

Jemidar Ali Bux, for it was that noted individual who spoke, now sat down, and invited Hoossein to partake of breakfast, an invitation gladly accepted by a young man who for some time past had been fed by little bits, stealthily conveyed to him at uncertain hours of the day or night. His escape was a great topic of conversation; the men had heard of the fact, while Hoossein supplied some of the details.

"Yes!" remarked an elderly man, with what was intended to be a grin through his hair development; " there is a quantity of fine young food thrown away to the fishes and pigs out of those upper windows; and the blue spirits of the departed are often seen rising from the old unused wells in the garden. If I was a stranger I would as soon sit down to dine with our Jemidar Saheb as go inside those high walls."

This little bit of sentimentality provoked much laughter.

While they are engaged in their morning meal let us take a more critical view of the men into whose society Hoossein was thus strangely thrown.

Ali Bux is a fine, handsome, muscular man, some fifty years of age; his deep sunken eyes are quiet now, but when any remark is made they twinkle in their dark recesses, showing that they can act at a thought's notice, and that they can on occasion become balls of fire; his moustache and beard are black as jet, curled and combed to perfection, and falling in graceful profusion half way down his expanding chest; his dress is scrupulously neat; the pugree of white muslin has a little fringe of gold tissue hanging jauntily over the left shoulder. The peculiar swagger of it was well known and much envied by the young copyists of Delhi and Lucknow. His angrica, of the finest long cloth from Manchester, was beautifully embroidered on the breast; there are little button holes sewn with golden thread, and little golden knots to fasten them with; they are open now, and disclose an emerald green silk vest, fitting tight to the body; his waist is loosely girded with a rich green fabric from Cashmere; his faulty legs are clothed in red satin pijamas, fitting tight, with many wrinkles below the knees. His feet have on a pair of white cotton stockings, and a pair of red gold embroidered slippers complete the costume of an unexceptionable Mussulman gentleman, starting on a pleasure trip of some six months' duration, for the unconcealed purpose of murder and robbery; the instruments for which, concealed carefully within his kumer bund, consisted of two roomals, some fragments of bone and pottery for Jadoo, and a well worn set of Chinese puzzles; a stock in trade, small, simple, but effective. Curiosity, mystery, and gambling attract most people in all parts of the world; but in case they failed Ali Bux was provided with song, dancing, and music; the web of the spider was woven with care, and flies were expected in plenty.

The rest of the party are chiefly nice looking young men, neatly dressed, with some swagger about them, betokening a life of easy indolence. The elderly man whom I mentioned above was the most ordinary looking fellow of the lot. He was neither well looking nor well dressed, but he was a person of some consideration; he was a wag and a story teller, improvisatore, that delight of Asiatics. His very looks made strangers smile, and he was honoured with the name of Seuliman Hadji, to denote his sanctity and wisdom. All were armed with some weapon or another, and it appeared by the conversation that the ostensible occupation of the company was the protection of a lady of high rank, who occupied, with her attendants, several bullock carriages, and who was bound on a pilgrimage to some distant shrine.

It may be instructive here, as showing the advantage of English officers looking into details in person, shortly to explain how I became acquainted with this lady.

Being on a hunting excursion on the borders of the province entrusted to my care, I one day fell in with several neatly dressed men, who were as unexpectedly there as I was. On enquiring to whom they belonged, they replied,

" To the Baiza Bhaè."

"Who?" I said; "to the Baiza Bhaè Scindia?"

"Ho, Sahib!" was the reply.

Now I knew her highness well, and believed her to be at that moment in a far distant part of the country, so I sent a message to the lady, whose camp was not far off, asking if I might come and pay my respects to her. The reply was that she would have had much pleasure in seeing me, but that she was travelling in haste, with no sufficient equipage to do honour to my kindness; but hoped soon to see me again at Nassick. Acting on secret information which my messenger picked up, I sent a police party to request the Baiza Bhaè to pay me a visit, as I had something of consequence to tell her. A refusal was not attempted, and she came; well dressed, deeply veiled, and well attended, the lady entered my presence. There was some tittering behind me, as after I had gravely paid her highness the usual compliments, I took the liberty of begging her to unveil. It was a difficult business, so she was assisted, and exposed a wrinkled face and skinny arm, very unlike those of the fine old lady who received the respects of Arthur Wellesley on the battle field of Assaye.

"You have been very ill, I fear. You are much changed," I said, gravely.

The old woman shook violently. I called forward an officer of police, who said before the assembly,

"This woman's name is Seu. She was once a dancing girl, then an attendant on them, then a fruit and opium seller at Nuggur, which place she left several years ago. Do you not recollect me?" he said to the lady.

I did not wait for an answer—it was evident how the case stood; so, as I had no information of any criminal act, I dismissed the party with a hint that they had better keep out of my district.

To continue my tale, Hoossein was called

aside by Ali Bux, and after a long conversation it was settled that our young friend was to be one of them in a tour of the provinces of Western India.

It was jokingly said by Seuliman Hadji, that they never started with a better omen, since they now had with them a man who had escaped from the clutches of Shitan in Jehannum itself.

The fraternity started; their little tent was pitched on some river bank, beneath some shady tree, by some charitable well, near gardens, or by mango groves. All the tricks of the profession were practised, and soon Hoossein saw the unwary travellers falling lifeless on the ground; he helped to plunder and to bury them in their shallow graves, and to conceal the spot by a fire made upon it. In the course of time he was admitted to the full privileges of the society, and the fatal roomal was concealed in his girdle.

"My nativity is true," thought Hoossein.

For two or three years these pilgrimages

continued; the Golgotha of Punderpoor was visited, the corpse paved banks of the Kishna; and Hoossein's last victim floated away on the flooded stream of the Seena; either that body was found, or some one gave information. The gang was captured; Hoossein consented to become an approver.

Ali Bux, with five more, were hung, and their sculls were sent to a Phrenological Society in England, which reported them to have belonged to good-tempered, harmless men. It was observed at the time that bumps arise on men's heads by knocking againt the obstructions of the law; hence, if Thugs do murder under the sanction of a Divinity, they have nothing to knock against.

I made Hoossein's acquaintance as an approver under Captain H——, at Poona, where, after dinner conversation gave me some of the outlines of my sketch; and where I submitted my neck to his manipulations, with a satisfied conviction that a gentle twist of his thumb and fore finger would have freed my spirit from this tenement.

Soon after this, the Thug department was closed, the approvers were discharged on surveillance, an existence by no means suited to our young friend, who will turn up next under very different circumstances.

CHAPTER V.

THE INVOLUNTARY MIGRATION.

The evening was warm, the house was disagreeable, and the room was low and long. Its dingy, yellow washed walls, were hung round thinly with pictures, chiefly of ships in full sail, with flags of all nations flying in the breeze, and the white spray flakes flying merrily over the bounding prows. The floor was boarded, and plentifully strewed with yellow sand; the windows were all open from top to bottom, from floor to ceiling. It was dark outside, but several oil lights, suspended by wires, threw a hazy light over as strange a group of human beings, as that dirty region of Calcutta ever beheld.

The company consisted of Chinamen, Malays, Indians, Portuguese, Dutch, Americans, English, Spaniards, Austrians, and French. Their language was a sound of utter confusion, yet an understanding was maintained in this mixed society.

An elderly negro sat on the floor by one of the windows, holding close converse with a fine-looking Arab seaman. There was a good deal of smoking going on; and the long table was covered with the remains of a meal; while glasses, full and empty, stood about in plenty.

A broad-faced Dutchman was boasting in a rollicking way of his good ship the, ——

"'Slow and sure' was her motto; there was many a ship passed her on the wide ocean, but none of them ever got to port before her; and as for her emigration business, why, there was her picture before them, crowded with fine young men, going from Calcutta, to make fine fortunes in the West Indies. Then, she was the ship to sail in—well found, never lost a rope yarn, a sail, or a sailor; and as to coolies, why they would die out of spite now and then; but while other ships, as he knew of, had lost half their cargo, she never lost but a dozen or so. There's old Hevelead, our captain, as jolly a skipper as one would wish to see; puts things to rights before-hand, knows when the storm is coming, and makes all snug; puts the passengers down below, and battens down the hatches to keep'm dry, he does; then brings her head up to wind under a storm sail, lashes the helm, takes a bottle to bed with him, and smokes till it's quiet again. Few skippers like old Hevelead; here's his good health, and luck to him. Grog tub always open, and such grog," said the seaman, as he took a pull at his glass.

"A regular trump," was remarked by

several dusky-looking men, and many said they should like to sail with Captain Hevelead.

"You can do so if you like," said a thin, wiry Malay, with round eyes, that sparkled like diamonds. "I have the book here to fill up, with fifteen good hands—pay —— dollars a month, good messing, and grog every day; extra in stormy weather, and we make more of that than most ships. Blue Peter is flying; she'll sail with the morning tide; the launch will be at the Ghaut by midnight, and any man who enters shall have a passage down in her."

The book was put on the table, the Dutchman entered several names in it, and the Malay repeating "Twelve o'clock to-night, at the Ghaut," left the room.

"That fellow will run a muck some day, or my name is not Dan," said a curly-headed old negro, with one eye. "Look here, lads, when I was cook aboard the 'Lowgee Family,' I said to a Malay chap, when he asked me for a bit of baccy, 'cut up your cap and smoke it;' so he up with the red hot poker, and jams it into my eye—that's the one that's gone—and then dashes along the deck, knocks over the boatswain, sets fire to the mate, and before he was caught and put in irons, there was plenty of doctor's work. I never trusted those glittering eyeballs since —too much opium in them; however, I wish you all a good voyage, mates."

The mess room of the sailors' home was empty; some had retired to rest, some had got their chests, and had gone to the landing place.. The clock was striking twelve, tide was running up strong, and along with the ripple of the stream came the splash of heavy oars.

A large boat pulled alongside the Ghaut; several men jumped ashore, and disappeared in the darkness.

"Are you there, Ali?" said a gruff voice from the boat.

"Aye, aye, Saheb," was the reply.

"How many of them are there?" asked the same voice.

"A full cargo," was the laughing reply.

"Never mind," said another, "the more the merrier. We can stow away a nice lot; they weigh light, and they won't sink us with talking, I'll be bound. The worst part of it is getting them up the ship's side; some of them begin to get right about that time, and kick and roar like all the bulls of Basan."

"I suppose," remarked the first speaker, "that they would not be missed if one or two of the roarers fell into the river quite accidentally?"

"Ah!" was the reply, "we ain't over particular, but we don't often get into trouble in shipping them. It's done pretty well, and cheap into the bargain, since it's called a volunteer departure; besides, we want all we can get, as we are paid by the head."

"Why is it called a volunteer departure?" asked another voice.

"Oh! that's the proper title for it, else

they would not call it by that name in Exeter Hall," said one, with a significant shrug of his shoulders; "but I like them better than regular niggers from Benin; they have some civilisation, these oriental coolies, and don't quite poison a fellow when he gets into the hold to doctor them."

"So much the better for me," replied a voice, from a young man, who just then stood up in the boat.

"Sit down, doctor, can't you?" said a voice, sharply; "they are coming."

The conversation was stopped, by the clatter of many feet, coming down the steps. Several men cast the burdens they carried into the boat, and then a number of sailor-looking men jumped in, followed by Yemma, the Malay.

"Who are these, Yemma?" asked a voice from the stern sheets.

"Foremast! all right!" was the quick reply.

"Cast off!" And the heavy boat swung lazily into the thick and steamy darkness.

There was a tinge of light in the east, when she glided silently alongside a large ship, anchored in mid-stream. The cargo was quickly transferred; not one of the living bundles awoke—the drugs had done their work well; there was no kicking—no screaming.

"Where's the doctor?" asked the boatswain, as he scanned each individual coming on board.

No one knew, and Yemma, of the diamond eyes, said "he was not in the launch when he jumped in. All the captain's fault, for letting him come, on the plea of humanity—all humbug. I thought he did not like his berth; however, we have got his stores and his mate all right."

The launch swung slowly astern, the whistle sounded, the capstan was manned, the fiddle struck up, the sails, lightly flapping in the breeze of the morning, were sheeted home, the anchor was tripped, soon hanging on the cat head, and the good ship

———— sailed smoothly down the Hoogley, on the top of the ebbing tide.

The deck was a scene of utter confusion—ropes laying about, packages, chests, and bundles, of various sorts and sizes, were scattered here and there; amongst this chaos were figures of human beings, in varied attitude. Now and then one would move, or groan, then relapse into quietude. Soon several of them began to sit up, looking about—weak and incapable, they held their racking heads in fevered hands—got up, rolled about, and asked for water; then wondered where they were, and where they were going to.

Standing amazed, in this miserable group, is one we know, Hoossein Ben Hassan—the lineal descendant of the prophet, is here, a drunken man, and an involuntary emigrant coolie. How came he here? The tale is soon told, the business of approver had filled his pockets from many sources—an accusation of Thugism was worth buying off; but when his occupation ceased, finding that his old companions looked coldly on him, and wishing to change his abode, he resolved to go to Calcutta, and set up in some honest occupation, so he coaxed Yusuff, with his wife and daughter, Ameena, to go with him, with full intention of completing his betrothal to the latter as soon as he was settled, and well rid of his former associates. With this resolve, he had reached the City of Palaces, and the crimps fell in with the sanguine young stranger; hence his racking head and his terrible situation.

Hoossein was awe-struck; he knew that something dreadful had happened—his senses still wandered—he was not quite sure that he did not dream; but the sounds, and the language around him, were strange—the scene was new; the tall masts, the big sails, the deck, the ropes, the confusion, all tended to convince him that he was, unfortunately, awake. Then, a peremptory order for him to go below, convinced him that he was not even his own master. He was told that he was a coolie; he declined to believe this—it was a catastrophe he could not as yet realize, till the darkness of the hold, the stench, his own language around, and the common tale of all, led him to believe it true.

It was not Hoossein's nature to despair. As health and strength returned, he bestirred himself to do something. A certain number of coolies were allowed to come on deck at a time; he saw that escape was out of the question, so he endeavoured to make himself useful. There were some English sailors on board; they befriended him, chiefly because he looked on his situation with the eye of a fatalist—calm under all circumstances, undisturbed by the distress and frenzy around, and quite confident that whatever was, must be endured.

Hoossein had heard Yusuff talk of the horrors of his pilgrim ship; but he had not realised them, and thought that the Hadji had taken the license of a traveller, and imposed on his youthful credulity. Those second-hand troubles appeared small and trivial, to those around him; yet the knowledge that others had suffered sorrows on the ocean, and had survived to tell the tale, enabled him to bear with greater equanimity those which overtook his miserable ship.

Before they had been a week at sea, cholera, small pox, and deadly fevers raged amongst the unhappy coolies. Sad at heart, unused to the sea, and with every element of evil around them, it was not to be wondered at if they fell victims to any disease that afflicted them.

There was an individual on board called the doctor, a young half caste, very boyish-looking, but calling himself twenty years of age. He had tumbled up quite accidentally —first in camp life; then he had gathered a little reading and writing, and got into an office under Government, before competitive examinations were invented. It was not in the lad's nature to sit down for twelve hours in the day, as his companions, the native clerks, did, to copy difficult writing, so he threw up the situation in disgust, and when tired of doing nothing, he obtained occupation in an indigo factory; but the work required of him not being congenial, he stayed for a short month, and then coaxed himself into a lawyer's office, where he picked up various fragments of knowledge, one of which was, that if he could only reach England, he would find a quantity of money waiting for him. While pondering on this subject, an advertisement, requiring a doctor's assistant, on board an emigrant ship, bound to the West Indies, met his eye—all expenses paid. He knew enough of geography to understand that the West were nearer to England than the East Indies, so he offered his services, which were at once accepted by the doctor, who, as he had made up his mind not to go himself, did not care who he got to assist him; so, as this gentleman had slipped away in the darkness and confusion at the

Ghaut, our young friend, Harry, found himself in sole charge of the ship's crew and passengers, some three hundred souls, all told. The captain cheered him up, shewing him all the medical stores and comforts, carefully provided by the contractor, and slapping him on the back, said, " Why, it will make a man of you."

The situation was enough to alarm a young fellow, who had no more experience of illness than the curing of a bad headache on hard working days had given him. But Harry took it calmly; he had been brought up in a rough way—no sympathy had been wasted on his childhood, so that he felt little for anyone else. As for the crew, he thought they could take care of themselves; and as for the coolies, why, as they were allowed to go from a country where they were wanted to one where—he could never understand why—they were not; and as many of them had come on board in a very promiscuous fashion, evidently unthought of and uncared for, he naturally concluded them to be unworthy of much consideration from him; his philosophy, indeed, carried him so far, that he actually imagined that coolies were born to suffer; and having arrived at this conclusion, he thought it quite right that the captain should make as much money as possible, by giving the smallest quantity of food; and that his own precious self should go on to England as pleasantly as possible, while the cargo died off like cattle, smitten by the murrain.

Under the influence of these feelings, Harry measured out the cholera mixture by the rule of thumb, put the small-pox patients overboard as quickly as possible, and handed over fever cases to his assistant Hoossein Ben Hassan, who administered mercury and quinine with the greatest discrimination and industry.

Hoossein had worked himself into this situation by his wonderful experience in corpses, making himself very useful to Harry.

He was rather dreaded by his companion Coolies, who gave him the title of the "Great Medicine," which stuck to him for many years.

A volume might be written on the miseries and atrocities committed and endured on that voyage; but as my hero is not likely to be much beloved for his conduct, I will leave the horrors of the scene to be painted by vivid imaginations, and inform my reader that the result of the accidental and fortunate treatment by the medical gentleman, and his native Indian assistant, was highly satisfactory; for, at the end of a prolonged voyage of ninety days, after having been afflicted by Providence with those inscrutable diseases, cholera, small-pox, jungle fever, and other maladies; yet, by the greatest care, the number of coolies (a race peculiarly liable to die) was only reduced from two hundred and thirty-three to one hundred and forty-five, or an actual loss of eighty-eight, not quite one death in a day!

Under these circumstances, the captain received his certificate of good management, while Harry and Hoossein received something more substantial in consideration of their volunteering to perform extra work and their humane conduct; the ship retained the official character given to it by the Dutchman in the Sailors' Home.

As for the voyage in general, it was very similar to all voyages, where Captain Hevelead commanded. They fell in with a thunder storm off Madagascar, but all was made snug before hand; the captain observing, before he got there, that as no spot on the wide ocean saw so much damage to ships, he for one would take all reasonable precautions; this he said with a sly look at a large square bottle on his cabin table; the mate laughed, the gruff boatswain laughed, and Hoossein, who did not quite comprehend the joke, went off into fits of laughter, upon which Captain Hevelead thought him a clever fellow. The Malay did not run a muck, but attended carefully to his duties as quarter master. Nothing could exceed the punctuality of the voyage. At four hundred miles distance, the day of reaching Table Bay was announced; as fresh departures were desired, the island of St. Helena was nearly run down in the dark; Ascension was made exactly at the hour foretold; the rock of St. Paul turned up on the larboard just as the glasses were looking for it on the starboard bow; while looking out for Tobago, Trinidad was discovered. He kept extra looks out while sailing through the narrow seas, and as tornados were frequent, he got down his royal masts and took in his flying jib-boom; no one should say that he, Captain Hevelead, ever lost a rope yarn, when a little forethought could save it. So, in good time, the old ship sailed safely into the land-locked harbour of Kingston, Jamaica.

For some days before arriving, Hoossein had been busy with a long, thin canvass bag; he borrowed the sail-maker's needle, finished off the work with a strap and buckle, and while all the eyes in the ship were looking at the charming scene before them, he filled the bag with what he called the funeral charges, fastened it carefully round his waist, and considered himself lucky in discovering that the trade of a doctor was better than that of a Thug. He was lost in a train of thought on this subject, his elbows resting on the bulwarks, when he was aroused by the flutter of many wings above him; he looked up, a flight of swallows passed over.

"My nativity is true again. I am a swallow!"

Before closing this chapter, I will venture a remark on coolie emigration, which, though managed better now than in the days of which I write, still occasionally furnishes dreadful tales of loss by shipwreck, or by disease.

How was it that emigration was ever permitted from the British Empire in the East? True, there is a large population, and famines are frequent local visitors; but there are large tracts of food producing lands only requiring inhabitants to convert them into use from the jungles which now occupy them; great works are sometimes stopped from insufficient labour—works that would benefit the people, and enrich the government; the price of labour in India has more than doubled within the last twelve years; yet, in the face of this great demand for labour on the spot, we have suffered many thousands of able-bodied men to leave a country where they were and are wanted, to go to other regions (from whence only a small proportion return) to satisfy a demand for labour created by our own mismanagement.

CHAPTER VI.

THE ASIATIC LEARNS A LESSON FROM THE AFRICAN.

It is of no consequence to my tale how the fusion of Asiatics and Africans took place in so distant a land from their respective abodes as the islands of the West Indies; there are curious natural currents in the ocean and in the atmosphere, but there is no current so strange as this artificial one made by man. I trust to be excused for diverging a little from my path up the fertile vale from which my stream is flowing.

We have reached Jamaica, a lovely island, remarkable for its sugar, its rum, and its yellow fever. England obtained possession of it accidentally: Oliver Cromwell was very anxious to take St. Domingo, but as that was not to be had, his admiral and general captured Jamaica from the Spaniards in the year 1655. Since then the island has been afflicted with many troubles. There have been earthquakes, tornados, floods, yellow fever, cholera, insurrections, fires, and emancipation; even since I began to pen this tale, there has been another plot, another rebellion, and another Nemesis allowed in a man fitted for the occasion.

Notwithstanding these frequent drawbacks, Jamaica was a very desirable possession; no soil was more productive, few productions more lucrative. We found a slave population on it, and as slavery was not very objectionable in those days, we used it to supply the agricultural demands; and for many years the old stock of slaves left by the Spaniards was replenished by fresh importations from Africa.

When opulence and trade in due time attracted attention to the locality, it was discovered by those who had no self-interest in it, that the slaves were badly treated; that they were whipped, scantily fed, uneducated, and utterly demoralised. It was a fine opportunity for the display of pure philanthropy; so fine speeches were made, and a large quantity of agitation was supplied to get the English nation into a proper sense of liberality and propriety—the one in reference to interfering with matters not belonging to them; the other only extending to a shadow, called compensation, for serious losses caused by the emancipation of the slaves, which Great Britain, in her pride and authority, effected.

So sanguine were the good people who carried this point, in the righteousness of the cause, and the humanity of the act, that they hoped and expected the inhabitants of central Africa would benefit by the occasion; but, unfortunately for them, the old curse still held good, and the negro was still to be "a servant of servants" to other nations, so that the abolition of slavery, however grand it may sound in the history of the world, never has been effected, while the efforts to effect it have actually caused more inconvenience and distress to those it was intended to benefit. Population increased over the fertile territories, watered by the rivers running from the Mountains of the Moon; and as the slaves did not go off so quickly as they used to do, the King of Dahomey, still, like the uncovered cause of the first great curse, dressed up in the sanguinary costume of a cocked hat and feathers, sacrificed thousands for his amusement.

It is too late to lament his victims, or the less fortunate thousands who were sacrificed under the horrors of the middle passage;

neither can any good accrue from a dissertation on the justice or injustice of slavery; but I will venture one paragraph on the subject of the emancipation.

There was work to be done. It was done by slaves. These were emancipated; it was hoped they would work as free men; but they were incapable or unwilling to do so. After a time, labour was furnished by British subjects from East India. They served for a time, and then had the option of returning to their homes. Some died, some went back richer, and some, as we shall presently see, all the worse for the society they had met with.

I ask the question seriously—Did not England lose a great opportunity by this sudden emancipation? Would she not have done better to have held the slaves for a certain term of years, under a system of education and morality? Would not some of these men have returned to their native land more fitted to do good there, than when they left it? We send the coolies back to India, and we might have done the same with the negro. If he had elected to remain in the colony, he would, in many instances, have been found fitted for civilised society; instead of being, as late events have proved him to be, the same plotter and murderer, as his brother in Central Africa appears to be by the interesting travels of Sir Samuel Baker.

Whether England was right or wrong in emancipation, it is not my object to prove. One thing is certain—that the sweat was wiped away from the brow of the African, but not from that of the Asiatic; no good can come when idleness is encouraged in any one.

Again, would it not have been better to have laboured longer and more earnestly to obtain the consent of all nations to the abolition of slavery? By our hastiness we added much to the troubles of those unfortunates, who were the victims of the traffic; while we lost ground in public opinion, for declaring a thing accomplished, which was very far from being so. I fear that the vanity of old England hurried her into a step, which, though she may have regretted, she could not recall. There have been moments, when her sons have recoiled in horror at the disclosures of the slave trade on the coast of Guinea, on the Indian ocean, and in Central Africa; where, even now, cows and human beings are about equal in value; on the Indian ocean, where hundreds of human beings have rotted, and died together between the narrow decks; on the coast of Guinea, where whole cargoes of living negroes have been cast into the ocean of eternity, to prevent their being found on board the ship.

Our medical men, only a few years since, were accustomed to bleed their fever patients, the disease obtaining a most fatal character; under more gentle measures it is disarmed of its fatality. Is it too late to try other measures for the suppression of the slave trade? The bleeding principle has been tried long enough; our sailors are required elsewhere; and though our money, which is gone, cannot be recovered, yet smaller sums expended judiciously, would be of more use than the millions which have gone.

We left Hoossein, struck with the conviction that he was a migratory creature; while still thinking on the subject, he was accosted in his own language by a well-dressed Mahomedan, who gave his name Muckbar Khan. He was, he said, a steward, and after some conversation, Hoossein engaged himself as a mucuddum (an overseer) of labourers, for three years, on very considerable payment.

So Hoossein went on shore; he had no trouble about luggage, though he had some difficulty in making the clothes upon him hold together. There was nothing to be admired in Kingstown, except dust and dirt; everything seemed to be neglected, and Hoossein felt glad when they turned round and saw the town behind them. In front there was a beautiful region, rich in verdure, and charming in variety of colour. In a few hours he reached his destination, a large, tumble-down sort of a house, with wide, open verandahs, like some he had seen in the east. The windows were broken, and the place was empty. On one side were several small huts in little enclosures, all neatly kept. To one of these Hoossein was introduced as his own; it was provided with everything necessary, but there was a difficulty about his clothing. A Derzi on the establishment soon fitted him out, and our hero found himself with a well filled girdle on his hips, in a snug abode, with some sixty coolies under him, all of whom were, in the course of a few hours, his most obsequious slaves.

The Bengali gave him little presents for concealing what he considered his little delinquencies; the Mussulman gave him contributions for the mosque and musjeed he intended to build, for their khubristan which he proposed to repair, and for the tazzia he was preparing for their grand festival of the Mohurrum.

Hoossein had an acquisitive genius; he understood the policy of minute collections from those beneath him, and he never lost an opportunity of realising dustoori from those above him. Those under him found their advantage in pleasing Hoossein; and, as he found it paid well, he tried to please his master.

Their salaries were paid regularly, and a certain amount of work was to be done in a given time. Nothing else was cared for; no moral influence was exercised. Their moolahs and their priests had not come with them; a few of the outward signs of their respective religions were attended to, but the rules of caste were laid aside. Most of them discovered that rum was sweet, and there was no synod to denounce the offenders.

As a body, the so-called coolies were a deceived set. False representations, drugs, and force had been employed to obtain them. They felt they were victims, so did not consider it necessary to be honest. They knew that as long as they could work they would get paid; but health and life were little thought of, and the only improvement to be found in those who survived the course of life up to the period of their return, was in their pocket, and this not so much the result of their own pay, as from gambling, or picking and stealing from their deceased friends.

Hoossein having fulfilled his three years to the satisfaction of his employers, but with a weary monotony to himself, declined to continue his service, and accepted the invitation of an old negro (one Sambo), who lived amongst the hills, to be one of them; "wa are a happy party," said the old fellow, with a grin, "plenty of sleep!"

After several days of lazy travelling, the new friends entered a sunny vale in the eastern part of Jamaica, through which a small rivulet ran into the Yellahs river.

Jutting into this vale was a little spur from the mountains. They slowly climbed the gentle ascent; there were beautiful hills, and thick forests above, and before them; on the plateau close to them was a cluster of huts, with men, women, and children sitting, or sauntering about; around were some small pretensions to cultivation, and behind stretched the magnificent, but neglected valley, stretching in its richness to the distant sea.

Hoossein sat down to look at the scene, rich and glorious. All around were the ample gifts of nature—a garden of Eden, tilled by the careless hands of those who once were slaves, who in their servitude had not acquired industry or ambition, who were content to cultivate only to such extent as was necessary, and that consisted chiefly in restraining wild luxuriance; yet the simple wants of the colony were gratified. Their ostensible occupation was agriculture, but work came only by fits, and starts; they had but few dealings with the outward world, and those only when clothes or other things were wanted, which their fruitful valley did not supply. Time was passed basking in the sunshine, card playing, drinking, smoking, and an occasional fit of religious enthusiam under the title of "Revival," a rare and spasmodic attack, dangerous if it had been frequent, more harmless as a little fragment of existence; they delighted in story telling, mythical legends of unrecorded generations, horrors only heard of in Africa, or from the lips of the African, things which would make a Christian weep, but which curled up the lips of the young negroes with a smile. Then there were later tales of blood to revel over, insurrections, earthquakes, hurricanes, and fires. The observations of a late traveller regarding them were very true; no sense of shame could be detected in them, they pilfered, and told lies, breaking the most sacred promises, resorting to violence without any occasion, laughing at torture; ignorant of science, sound, or colour, they would endeavour to paint and sing, and fall into fits of laughter at their absurd failures. They were savage, superstitious, and cowardly. They called themselves Baptists, not from any knowledge of the subject, but because they had been told to do so. It was a different title from the established religion of the white man, and something they thought was gained by the distinction.

Into this den of professed idleness and vice the oriental Mahomedan was now introduced, and soon found himself domesticated.

It was Hoossein's chief delight, when the gentle sea breeze blew softly through the overhanging bananas, when the luscious fruit hung down in clusters, wooing the appetite, to sit in a snug corner looking out upon the distant sea, with Sambo as his companion, exchanging tales of their atrocious adventures.

The only reason for supposing that Sambo was not personally engaged in the rebellion of the slaves in 1831, was that he said he had been; for the same reason, we may hope that the string of horrors which he drew from that event had no foundation in fact. He had a whole volume of dread tales, told in divers manners, to suit his audience, but his favourite theme was the destruction of the property upon which he had been employed as a child, where he had nothing to complain of but too much love and kindness, where he had a chance, if any slave ever had it, of being reclaimed from the wild jungle in which he lived, from the ferocity in which he revelled. Even after the lapse of many years his dull eyes rolled in excitement, as he recounted the burning of the homes of the store houses and the dwellings; he laughed aloud as he described the flight of the women and children from the fire; their capture by the slaves around, how the little ones were hurled, midst cries, imprecations, and entreaties, back again into the hissing and crackling flames; and the women were kept for insult and torment, the living victims of their drunken orgies, till in weariness of vengeance for no offence, they threw the sufferers, for a lingering and cruel death, in the smoking embers of their former happy homes.

Hoossein, too, had his adventures and his murderous experiences to amuse Sambo, and the old man eyed the young one as he would look on a divinity, as he told him how on one occasion the people to be strangled were more numerous than the stranglers; at his (Hoossein's) earnest solicitation the fatal roomal was entrusted to him, and a fair young girl was his allotted victim; no feeling of mercy no compunction at the destruction of youth and beauty, had any sway with him, but by accident he bungled in the execution; the girl saw all her friends killed before her face in an instant; she had time to think, and to turn an imploring look on her intended murderer—even to offer her innocent self as a sacrifice for her life, with a promise on her bended knees, with uplifted hands, of perpetual and inviolable secresy; "but," said Hoossein, with that hissing tone, denoting excitement, "I remembered my motto on the talisman, my dead father rose upon my memory, 'what thou doest do,' and so the roomal was readjusted, and she seemed to fall asleep."

Such were the common amusements of these congenial spirits. The negro was diabolical by nature, the Asiatic by accident. If he fell in with it, he did the evil; and so they killed the time, and fed on the fruits around them, the orange, the banana, the shaddock, and the pineapple; they drank rum, and soothed themselves with tobacco; the climate was luxurious, the scene around was beautiful, and existence was the very perfection of idleness.

Before Hoossein left India, he had neither experience nor the opportunity to judge of the English character; he had heard his father and Yusuff speak of them on the western coasts as great kings, just and energetic; he had himself fallen under the criminal laws in those provinces, for deeds which had been perpertrated in the central districts with impunity. It is true he had been conditionally pardoned, but what little respect he might have had for the authorities was not increased by this lenity, which like all orientals he considered a mistake. While he was in the Bengal provinces he seldom heard the name of an Englishman,— the native officials were the great men there; but yet his instinct taught him to consider the English as a great people.

It was a warm and a thirsty day, when Sambo undertook to correct this erroneous opinion.

"Great men!" said the sable philosopher, as he rose from his reclining position, resting his head on his hand; "they are not a great people; they never have been great, and they never will be great; they are a narrow minded, selfish race, jealous and distrustful; they are all traders, and will sacrifice everything for money. They always want a change, and never know when they are well off; they have strong laws, and they are called brave people, but they seldom take advantage of their bravery. Uncertain and vacillating, they will convict a man of murder, but decline to hang him. They send rascals to gaol, but let them out again to prey on the community." Hoossein winced. "Tell me," said the orator, warming on his subject, as he smacked his knee with his left hand, " would great men injure themselves by keeping engagements with nothing to bind them? would they ruin their friends for the chance of benefiting an alien? Psha! My master was better off when we were slaves, and we were better off also, but we frightened them into setting us free. If we gave them the chance," (and Sambo drew his fore finger across his throat), " they would make us slaves again. They can be frightened, and plagued into anything; they prefer lies and diplomacy to bloodshed and the sword;

they are bigotted and narrow minded; they have what they call a church, but dispute how to serve it; some are over religious, and some have no religion at all; they split straws, and make mole hills into mountains. Their king great, indeed! Ha! ha! he lets his subjects do as they like. If I was king I would hang all who did not pray as I did. We would soon see who was great then; this universal sufferance will be the ruin of them, and the sooner it comes the better. I only hope that I may live to see it. I hate them—I abhor them!"

Sambo foamed and raved. Hoossein looked at him with awe. The old man's eyes rolled in frenzy, his words came fast and strong, as he continued—

"Great people? I will exterminate them, I will! There is the sea, blue and calm; I will ruffle its smoothness into waves with their kicking, and turn its blueness into red with their blood."

He gnashed with his white teeth, and tore

with his thick fingers, as if pulling to fragments some detested thing; then suddenly subsiding, he seized Hoossein by the hand, and whispered, vehemently,

"Will you help us? There will be glory in the deed, and a recompense when it is done."

He waved his hand and said,

"See! all this shall be ours; we will turn them out of it. They took it by force; let them lose it by force. We have no home but this; we will keep it as our own, and you, you were stolen from your friends and your country. Does no feeling of revenge rankle in your breast? We are nearly ready to strike. Will you help us? or are you too silly to see, too timid to seize the opportunity?"

"Hold!" said Hoossein, calmly, "there is no opportunity now; there are soldiers in plenty, and you are scattered far and wide. You have no combination, or plan. You require unity, secresy, and determination.

You get excited when you ought to be calm. You talk and gossip, and are, therefore, unfitted to be plotters. If you beat the air while talking on the subject, what would you do when the moment for action arrived? I fear you are not to be trusted in so serious a matter."

"Enough," said Sambo, angrily; "I have found you out. You are as useless as a tortoise!"

"Ah!" thought Hoossein to himself, as he rose from his seat, "I am a tortoise, and have been so for two years. My destiny progresses!"

CHAPTER VII.

AMEENA.

WHILE Hoossein ekes out his time in Jamaica, we will take a look at those he left behind.

It was a sultry evening in the month of September, 18—, when an English cavalry regiment encamped on the bank of river, in front of a thick grove of mangoe trees.

The season was early for marching; but unusual things were transacting in those days. India enjoyed an unusual Governor-General, and political reasons of extreme moment existed as an excuse for exposing troops to unusual exposure. The monsoon was scarcely over, the jungles were wet and unhealthy, and the rivers were still deep, and rapid torrents.

As might have been expected, fever and cholera did make their appearance on the second day's march, but not to such an extent as to alarm the Colonel, who knew that the quicker he moved on, the sooner he would be out of danger. It was a favourite expression of his, "give men no time to be ill; keep up excitement," he would say to his surgeon. "I will give them excitement, and they will not require much of your medicine." And so it proved. Sickness was soon out-marched, and everything was going on as satisfactorily as the season would allow.

A large double-poled tent occupied the front centre of the camp; the flag of old England was too damp to flutter in the light breeze. A ten days old moon sent her fitful light on departing day, and shone on the white jackets of the servants, as they moved backwards and forwards from cook to tent. An Indian kitchen is a large one—the wide vault of heaven, a level sward, a ploughed field, a bare rock. A dinner fit for a king can be cooked with few appliances. A few stones form the fire-places; wood from the nearest jungle the fuel; this kitchen is only a few paces from the tent, and the dishes go in smoking hot.

By degrees the rapid circulation stops, the dishes have been brought out and washed and packed. Each servant takes off his master's service, and the lamp-light in the tent grows hazy under the clouds from Manilla cheroots.

Seated at the middle of the table was a stout, hale man, of ruddy complexion, with kind and twinkling light blue eyes. At the sound of the bugle he rose from his seat and said,

"Now, then, youngsters, good night. Off to your roosts. First bugle half-an-hour before cock-crow in the morning."

In a few minutes the tent was empty, and the Calassies were busy striking and packing it, to send it on to the next encampment.

One of the youngsters alluded to, Cornet Charles Eglington, did not go to roost; but bringing an easy chair outside his tent, sat himself down in it to finish his cheroot, and to meditate on the far-off home he had so lately left, with a pair of bright brown eyes, which still formed his beacon light.

His thoughts were very chaotic—full of bewildering fancies, like the confused ripple of the stream that ran before him, glittering in the moonbeams. He stood up and watched the silvery waters glide away. Where did they go to? where did they come from? and he would have thought on and on in a dreamy state incident to such a situation, had not his attention been attracted by strange sounds rising from the river—they sounded like groaning, weeping, and talking.

Charles walked in the direction of the sounds, and on reaching a turn of the river bank, he discovered a human being grovelling in shallow water, using wild gestures, and wilder speech, mixed with laughter and lamentation. He approached it: it was a native female, hanging over what appeared to be a corpse.

"He will not hear me," she cried; "he will not speak. Ibrahim! oh, Ibrahim!" she screamed, "come back—come back, to me! It is Ameena who calls you. The men are waiting for their water. Come! oh, come!"

Charles ventured to say that the man was dead.

"Oh! no—no—no—" she cried, without looking up, "he is not dead—he cannot be dead. He told me he would fetch the water, and come back. Get up, Ibrahim! Oh! do get up."

She pulled up the man's hand, which fell back with a dull, heavy splash in the passing stream.

G

"Dead! dead! then Ameena will go with with you. She will be your houri in Paradise. No one else shall pillow your head amidst the beautiful, the never-fading flowers."

"I come! I come!" she cried, and rushed out upon the moonlit stream.

Charles with all the eagerness of youth, and the courage of an Englishman, unheeding the depth or the rapidity of the river, rushed to the rescue, and soon drew the dripping girl to the shore. What was to be done? She was quite unconscious. He did not like to disturb the camp, by calling for aid, so, as she could not walk, he carried her to his tent and laid her on the bed. He thought she was dead, but as he watched over her, and had just determined to call the doctor, a strong spasm crossed over her, her breast heaved, her eyes opened and life regained its sway. Still she raved, and reason. was unseated. For some time Charles did not dare to leave her, till by degrees she became quiet. He then wrapped her in a blanket, and going to his chair sat in it, half sleeping, half waking, till the bugle sounded.

His adventure rose, misty and dream-like before him. "My situation is like the morning two hours before daybreak, cold and gloomy," he said to himself. He did not feel quite sure that he had not dreamed. His clothes, however, were still wet; he looked into his tent, "Ah! it is quite true," he muttered, "she is there." The oil light flickered on his table; he took it up and looked at her. What beautiful features! but they were nothing to him; he only thought of, what is to be done?

"By Jove!" he said, as a sudden thought struck him; "I will go and tell old Bones"— this was the familiar title of the regimental surgeon—"I dare say that good old soul will lend me a dooly."

So off he ran to his friend's tent.

"Hilloa, Bones!" he cried on reaching it. "Are you up?"

"Of course I am, and getting my beard off. Who are you, and what do you want?"

Charles explained that he had come for a dooly and bearers.

"Who is ill?" asked the doctor.

"A poor girl I found in the river last night."

"Ah! ah!" cried the doctor, in the intervals of his shaving. "Water nymphs, naiads, and mermaids. I will be over and see about it in a minute."

Charles was fastening on his sword when Bones came in.

"You are a nice young fellow," he began; but on looking at the pale, anxious face he spoke to, the doctor stopped, and after a moment's hesitation, he continued, "I have brought a dooly, so let me see the patient."

She still slept, and in that state was placed in the conveyance; a Mussulman servant was sent on with instructions regarding her, and Charles instituted inquiries on the subject.

He discovered that a bheestie (water carrier) was missing. He told the men where to find the body, but the stream had risen during the night, and it was not to be found.

The bugles sounded, the march began, and Cornet Charles Eglington attended to his duties.

The next camp was reached, the horses were picketed with head and heel ropes, they were groomed and fed, stables were over, and the officers went to breakfast.

Before they had finished this meal, which is a more important one in India than in England, an elderly native entered the tent; he was rather short, very black, with thin grey hair streaming out here and there under his turban, small piercing eyes, very little clothing, legs the very picture of muscular development, and a bamboo shafted spear in his hand.

This was old Duttoo, the well-known shikaree of the —— hunt.

He was at once greeted with smiles and questions.

" There are hogs ! " he said.

A general rise took place.

" Where ? How many ? Dant Wallah ? "

with many other questions, were put without obtaining answers.

Some familiar slaps were bestowed on the old man's back; tea was offered him, which he did not take, and brandy, which he did.

Then Duttoo said,

"They are on the move; they are almost in sight. I have left men watching them, and there, on yonder ground, is a man waving his pugree; quick, Sahebs, quick!"

Horses were ordered and saddled, hunting gaiters or boots pulled on, and in less time then I can write the tale, there were seven as gallant hunters as ever carried spear, cantering up the gentle slope to the signal man.

No one was more devoted to sports of all sorts than Charles Eglington; bred up in the routine of country life, he had learned hunting in Leicestershire, shooting in Norfolk, fishing in Scotland and Wales. His fishing tackle, guns, and spears were always ready, and although on this occasion he had some anxieties which he could express to no one, his good horse, Exmouth, was saddled, his long sambre skin gaiters were pulled on, and with light rein and lively heel, he cantered off as jovial as the rest.

The signal man was soon reached; he pointed out a small patch of Banbul jungle, into which, he said, the hogs had just gone. He advised a long detour to meet them, and so drive them back on to better ground than that which lay before them, where the cultivated lands would soon give the hog a chance of escape.

But "The Sounder Boar was on before," so at them at once was the order of the day. In the meantime the quick eared pig had taken alarm at the sound of horses' feet and the talking of man, and slipped off unseen. The tracks were soon found.

"Away! away!" shouted the leader.

Along the rugged banks of the broad water course, a long stern chase; above, the ground was rotten, full of large holes and thorny bushes. The bed of the ravine, strewed with rocks and boulders, was generally impracticable to horses.

After a gallop of a mile the chase was seen.

"Ride, boys! ride!" shouted Danvers, the secretary, who waived his glittering blade on high.

The old grey boar heard the sound and stopped; for one moment he glanced behind him on his pursuers, shewing his long white tusks " and his whiskers grey ;" one moment more he took to consider which way to go, and then the bristly beast ran right down the water course at a thundering pace, for his garden of Eden—the nearest sugar cane field.

Hot and furious rode the men on the banks of the ravine, with "tightened rein and bloody spurs," some on one side, some on the other ; on a sudden the boar took a small path which led to the left. Charles was the leading rider on that side ; he lowered his spear for the thrust, but just before him ran a deep sharp ravine, with thick bushes on either bank. There was no escape, he must go over or in. Exmouth jumped it clean, but stuck immovable in the thick, strong jungle on the opposite bank.

Young Skyman, riding on the other side of the water course, marked the turn of the boar, and crossing on his track, came up the pathway at racing speed, drawing first blood from the beast, as he passed close in front of Charles still entangled in the thicket.

As soon as the boar reached the open field he turned to bay. It was of no avail that his tusks gnashed, his eyes glared, and his mouth foamed; there were practised hand and bold steeds that never flinched, coming to meet him. Allegro and Mayday, Red Rover and Kremlin, all as daring as himself; and so he fell—that monster boar—with tusks eleven inches and a half long.

"Who will ride home and send out a tattoo for me?" said Charles, as he extricated himself "I fear Exmouth has broken down."

Skyman galloped away.

"Where are Fred and Danvers?" said some one.

"After the sows," was the reply.

And the rest of them rode back to see what more sport they could get. They had not gone far before they met men running, who said Danvers Saheb was killed; but it turned out that he was still at the bottom of a ravine, with his leg broken, attended to by Fred. No one knew him by any other name —though it may be supposed he had one, and he having volunteered to ride a friend's runaway horse, and being, as luck would have it, a strong rider, capable of holding an elephant, kept Guardsman well in hand, witnessed the catastrophe, and immediately assisted poor Danvers.

"It is not broken, is it?" he said, in reply to an exclamation from the latter.

"If it was not," said the poor fellow, "I could not feel the bones grating together inside my leg."

Fred immediately rode away, and sent off a man to camp, who, at the moment I have come to, was returning with the surgeon, Fred's servants, who thought their master was the injured person; and several troopers, all of whom were anxious to help their dearly beloved Fred Saheb. There was not a man in the regiment who would not have followed Captain Fred to perdition; they were sorry for Danvers, but there were signs of joy when they discovered that their pet officer was not the injured one.

As Danvers was now in safe hands, all but Fred rode away, returning to camp about tiffin time, with plenty of hog's flesh for chops, and the inevitable souse.

"Oh!" groaned the colonel, as he entered the tent, where beer mug was all the fashion, "a broken down charger, and a broken legged captain—a very serious hour's amusement! If it goes on like this there will be none of you left for the Afghans."

Looking round the horses was the next

thing to be done. Exmouth, that gallant silver grey, stood upon three legs; Wallenstein, the dun, with ebon points, writhed in pain from multitudes of long thorns in his limbs, over which a hot embrocation plaster of white ants' earth was being applied by careful grooms; Kremlin had fallen on his side, and was gashed by sharp rocks from shoulder to hock; Red Rover had been amongst the stones, a cut on his heel was being blown up with gunpowder, and his wounded fetlocks were washed with salt and water.

Skyman stopped with Exmouth, and thinking that something had been omitted, asked the horsekeepers where their master was; on being told in his tent, he went there. He was on the point of entering without ceremony; but as he was doing so he heard a female voice say,

"I must die; I have nothing left to live for—nothing upon earth."

The young man withdrew; but as he did so, he stepped on the surgeon's toes.

"That's right," said the latter; "that comes of hog and mug, and something has happened to Charles."

"Did he send for you?" said Skyman.

"I suppose he did," was the curt reply.

Skyman put it down to the corns, and walked away.

Whatever joke was ready, on the smiling face of the Doctor, as he pulled aside the perdah, was suppressed by a glance inside the tent.

"Mad—mad?" he asked.

"Yes, mad!" said Charles.

"Mad—mad! both of you," repeated the Doctor in tones of deep compassion.

He took the girl's burning hand in his, and said, quietly,

"Do you still wish to die?"

"Oh, yes!" she cried; "I must die directly. Ibrahim calls me often, and tells me to make haste; but they vex me, and say I must not die, that he can do without me; but that is impossible. May I not die, Doctor

Saheb? You are always good to poor Ameena."

"Yes; you can go if you like. Paradise must be much pleasanter than this world," said the Doctor.

"How good, how kind of you. Ibrahim will thank you, and he shall be your water carrier, and will bring it cool and sweet for you. What a nice bungalow you will have, when you go there, Doctor Saheb; such punkahs and such mirrors," and Ameena laughed a delirious laugh.

"Now then, take this," said the Doctor, holding a glass of liquid to her mouth; "this will send you to Paradise."

"Will it?" said the girl, eagerly seizing it.

"Yes," said the Doctor; "you will go there so pleasantly."

She swallowed the draught.

"Now," said Bones to Charles, "leave your tent standing to-morrow; Saturday your man can come on with it, and catch us on Sunday. In the meantime pig with me. I will leave an old woman to look after her; but, my boy, you must send her away."

Charles felt uncomfortable, as he muttered, "Oh! of course I shall."

The Sunday morning service was never omitted by Colonel ———, and as Charles left the tent where it was held, he saw that his own tent had been pitched. He walked towards it, feeling an unknown tremour passing through him. He entered. Ameena was seated on the ground; the tremour passed over him again. He spoke—she arose, and said she was better.

Charles was astonished at the perfection of beauty he saw before him. A plain red saree hung over the head, and enveloped the whole body; its lines of symmetry were visible under the soft texture of her dress; her ebon hair escaped on one side; her forehead was higher than usual for an oriental, with high arched eyebrows; the eye lashes were long, nearly concealing the timid glance which she cast on the young man. He shunned the look, yet he knew the look was given, and he felt that those lustrous black eyes looked kindly on him.

She knew but little of what had passed; but she was better, and they stood for a few moments not knowing what to do next; he incapable of saying go!

Then she spoke in trembling accents. She almost wished she had been allowed to go to Ibrahim; but she was told that she owed her life to a good and brave young man; she was told that she ought to feel grateful; but her life was of so little value that her gratitude was too small to express. She could only give her simple thanks to him for doing what was good and humane, and she hoped God would reward him for doing his duty to a fellow creature, however undeserving of it; as for her future, as Providence had so willed it that she should not die, she would be content to trust in God for the future.

Her effort was over, and she relapsed into gentle sobbing.

Charles Eglington had no experience in these

things. He tried to calm her, but got confused himself; he expressed his sympathy with her sorrow in such Hindoostanee as he could muster. He could not tell her to go. He had never spoken an unkind word to anyone—it was not his nature to do so; he was not selfish; he thought that she would go of her own accord. He had indeed thought she would go; but she did not. She waited to be told to go; he waited for her to do so. There was an acknowledged sympathy, which prevented either from acting; their very natures assimilated.

She was as soft and gentle as a child; she had obeyed, respected, and attended to her husband; no voice sang as sweetly as hers, when the women sat down at the grinding; no smile was more joyous than hers, as she prepared the mid day repast for her husband; in fact, she was very cheerful, and took things pretty much as they came. She was very young and very innocent. She had never acted for herself, so she staid where she was. She would not have liked to go, for there was kindness and attention around her, which she had never before experienced; there were congratulations on her good luck, and hopes that she would befriend them, when she could. Ameena had got into a new atmosphere; it was not unpleasant; she did not know it was unhealthy, and so Ameena staid in the tent of the Englishman.

CHAPTER VIII.

ENGLISH OFFICERS.

THERE are tides in the affairs of man—the flood and the ebb; there are currents and eddies in the lives of all. Few attend to them, or if they do, they commonly pass them over, with the observation, " a narrow shave that!" or, " what a bit of luck!"

A little whirlpool in existence is contained in the following narrative; but the impression it made on the real actor in the scene was not lightly looked on, his salvation was considered as coming direct from Providence, for the intent and purpose that his life might be occupied in doing good.

Some days have passed away. The march was resumed early on one Monday morning; the route lay through a thick grassy country, reported to be full of game. The white tents of the encampment were just visible on a rising ground, some four or five miles distant, when the Shikarees brought intelligence to the officers of a marked down tiger.

Permission having been obtained, Fred, Charles Eglington, and several others, taking their guns and rifles, went off with the Shikarees. On reaching the place, they inspected it with anxious eyes; it was a flat, bushy locality, cut up by ravines, on the edges of which was generally a tangled jungle; while below the grass was thick and rank—here and there was a stunted tree.

The spot was a dangerous one, and some time was occupied in a careful examination of the ground, before deciding on the plan of attack; but when the well-practised and cool sportsman, Fred, told Eglington to come with him, and directed the others to various points, with cautions to take care of themselves, matters looked progressive.

A few beaters, who had been arranged by the Shikarees, were now signalled to advance from the upper end of the ravine, in which the tiger was supposed to be.

There was a sudden yelling of discordant voices in that quiet and secluded vale—tom toms began to beat, and tin utensils to jingle; then came the crackling of squibs, as, tied to stones, they were lighted, and thrown into likely bushes—nearer and nearer came the men, full of excitement—louder and more incessant came the shouting and the din. On a sudden, a shot was fired, and up came, from the thick grass, the well-known rattle of a tiger's roar.

Fred, touching Charles on the shoulder, pointed to a thicket below them. At the same moment Charles fired. There was a quick, sharp growl, from an unseen beast, and the long grass waved and bent, as an animal rushed through it, at speed, and then all was silent. The beaters had retired—some were perched on the little trees, some had gone away as quick as possible; while the well-trained Shikarees had collected, for mutual protection, on a plot of bare rock.

No one saw where the tiger had gone to; he had not gone past a certain spot; but the cover was thick and impervious, so that he might be anywhere.

Skyman, who had fired the first shot, which gave him a title to the skin, went with another young man to the spot where he shot at the tiger. The closest inspection found no blood. They then went to where the last shot was fired, and following the tracks for a few yards, blood was found on the broken blades of grass; but tracking was voted dangerous in that thick cover. They thought of the beaters; but Fred called out that not a man should go into that place, where they were afraid to go themselves.

The young men, with their servants, and some Shikarees, then made as close a search as they could, without success. The midday sun was getting hot, they had had no breakfast, and it was voted a bad job.

Fred and Charles had to cross a small branch ravine, to join the rest of the party. While doing so, Fred stepped aside to examine a likely-looking thicket, at a short distance. Charles went on; but just as he had climbed the bank, he heard a roar, a shot, and a rush behind him. He looked back, and saw the tiger in the very act of springing on his friend. There was a moment of shaking and tearing, and then the gun rose steadily to his shoulder—the trigger was pulled, and the bullet sped; but the beast still lay upon his friend. There was an instant of time, in which Charles thought, " Shall I fire again? if I do I may kill Fred." Still, he was on the point of firing, when the yellow tiger, sleek and glossy, rolled over, and the man arose. Where was his cap?—still crunched in the animal's mouth; a small trickle of blood ran down Fred's cheek.

"Thank God!" said Fred, as he picked up his old Joe Manton; "that was a good shot of yours, Charles, and the old gun is not much hurt. Look here! as I fell, I held it across the brute's mouth; his teeth have left their mark on the stock and the rib." (The gun bears the mark to this day.)

On examining the tiger, they found one shot through the spine, which gave him the death wound, at the very instant his tooth had penetrated through the thick cap, a silk handkerchief, and the skin of Fred's head. There was another wound on the hip; and as that was on the side from which Charles had fired his first shot, the skin was awarded to him; but he laughed at the idea of having it, and insisted on Fred keeping it. "Of course," he said, "the skin will be an accompaniment to the wondrous tale of your escape. And oh! how thankful I feel, that I was allowed to be the humble means of your delivery."

The two men squeezed one another's hands — a more expressive action than words, and all the party trotted on to camp.

Pale and uneasy with the new excitement he had just endured, Charles entered his tent. Ameena was there; and her woman's wit was already calming the over-worked feelings of the young man, when the doctor entered the tent, to enquire, as he said, about the tiger accident, of which strange rumours were already circulating in camp.

"Yes," said Charles, "it was a strange thing; I scarcely know now how it all happened. I thought I might kill Fred; but I knew the tiger would if I did not shoot, and God guided my aim. I was never more astounded and delighted, than when Fred kicked the beast from off him."

"Ah!" said the good doctor, "that is an

event which you will never forget while the pulses of your heart beat. To retain your senses, calm and manageable, when the life of a fellow creature depends on that calmness, is one of those gifts, so touchingly described by the 'Path finder.' We all have gifts of sorts, seldom discovered, till accident displays them. There is," said the doctor, hesitating a little, as if to collect his ideas from the tiger scene, "a gift, which, of all others, is most essential to the young man, as he first enters on the scenes of life. If I had been possessed of it, I should not now be speaking to you. It was because I had not the gift of denial that I am here. Then again, none of us can look into futurity; and if I had said 'no,' I might not have been of the same service to my fellow creatures, as I have been. Listen to me, young man, for a few moments;" and the doctor rubbed his hard hand across his eyes. "She was not beautiful—she was not young; but she was very kind to me, and I was grateful to her.

I had not then known what real love was. She thought I loved her; and when her brother spoke to me on the subject, I could not say that little word, ' no.' The day was fixed for making me a rich bridegroom, with every worldly comfort about me. I accepted the congratulations of my friends, on my escape from the army, to which I was destined. I thought it would be very pleasant to do nothing all my life; but the day before the wedding, poor Anne was taken ill, it turned out to be the small pox, and she died. The time for my commission had passed away, my chance of wealth was gone, and nothing was left but to work. It was up hill all the way, till I took to the study of medicine; that suited me, and here I am. I have been behind hand all my life; I hope I am not too late now. I have—though I ought not to say so—been useful to more than one young man, and I feel happy, when such opportunities come before me, to do my best for my fellow-creatures. I am willing to try now; and should be only too glad if my effort is successful. Can I induce you, Charles Eglington, to use the gift which I had not. Will you say no?" The old man's voice trembled; but he continued, in a low and earnest tone, " say no, man; and say it soon." He laid his hand on the young man's shoulder, and again repeating, " say it!" he strode hastily away.

There was something on Charles' mind which weighed heavier than the kind, fatherly advice of the surgeon. He remembered the parting with his much loved mother, and the words she whispered in his ears while embracing him for the last time. They were lost upon him then, and passed like the summer breeze, but now the whisper again sounded in his ear, and he understood the meaning of "Charles, have nothing to do with native women." He resolved to act upon them, and obey his mother.

It was night ; a small light flickered in his tent. Ameena reclined upon a carpet, Charles knelt beside her, and taking her small hand in his, he said,

"You are well now, Ameena; you must go!"'

Ameena's face fell upon his hand as she said,

"Go? What for? What have I done? Where can I go to? Oh, let me stay; do not, send me away now."

"It is not right that you should stay," he said.

"Aha!" she cried. "Not right? Why not? Why did God save me? Why were you sent to the rescue; you alone of all the thousand men that slept within the hearing of my calls? If it is not right for me to stay, it was not right of you to save me, or to take care of me, or to call the doctor to me."

"My coming was an accident," he said; "and all the rest was common humanity due to any one of God's creatures."

"No! no! it was no accident!" she cried. "Was it accident that brought you into the world? Was it accident that sent you to India? Did you save your friend from the tiger by accident? Tell me, Eglington Saheb," she said, slowly, and firmly looking him full in the face, "why was I saved by you?"

Charles was no casuist; there was a temptation before him, but he scarcely saw the danger; his was not the time of life to look to consequences; the arguments used were plausible, and carried him away from the main point, so, in a careless tone, he said,

"I do not know!"

"I know!" cried Ameena. "It was your kismut and my kismut."

Yes! It was the kismut of that Mahomedan woman to live in the tent of the Christian.

Time slips on; the quiet routine marches through a friendly country are over; the Indus river has been crossed, the arid wastes of Scind are left behind, the Balan pass, with its wild and rugged mountains, has been passed in safety, and the rough country of Affghanistan has been gained.

History tells how gallantly the Bombay column held its own, and upheld its glittering name; but my tale confines itself to individuals. The regiment I am speaking of formed a portion of that army, and though I must sometimes embrace historical subjects, I shall, as far as possible, confine myself to my tale.

One day, just as the march was finished and the men were getting the morning meal, an alarm was raised that the grass cutters of the regiment had been attacked, and cut up by the Affghans.

There was a saddling in hot haste, a buckling on of spurs, and a girding on of swords. In a few minutes three hundred men were galloping away to avenge the slaughtered foragers; for five long miles they galloped on, and still no foe was seen; the horses were getting fatigued, for they had gone through a long march, had no time for feeding, and now their greatest strength was needed.

A few dead bodies of grass cutters were found, stripped and mutilated; the perpetrators of the slaughter of these unarmed men were invisible, but a small flag fluttered in the breeze on a neighbouring hill; towards this the commanding officer led his men.

As they approached the foot of the hills, they became gradually alive with men, wild hill men, mounted on their small but active horses, armed with matchlock, spear, and falchion, as formidable an enemy as could well be met with.

Fred took the liberty of suggesting to the Colonel that the horses should be rested, or that a feigned retreat should be made, so as to entice the enemy into the plain. He was not attended to, but on they went, and the bugle sounded the charge.

Up the steep hill the gallant horses labour hard; their fatigue, the broken ground, destroyed the line, and the charge could not be completed.

The wild foe watched their opportunity; their country, their homes, their freedom were at stake; they were on their own hill side; fierce and strong, down they came on the disorganised cavalry like an avalanche from the mountains; the attack was irresistible, individual bravery was of no avail, the clattering torrent could not be stopped, and quicker than the description of the misfortune a hundred saddles were emptied.

Ravenswood and Moncton were down; several other officers, Eglington amongst them, were wounded; the troops, no longer in control, sought safety in flight, while Fred alone, calmly and slowly, came down the hill with a heavy heart. These men whom he had so often led on to victory, were now routed and disorganised, and it was not their fault.

Fred found himself almost alone; he diverged a little from the line of pursuit, in which the Affghans were now collecting their plunder, in which occupation, others who were near him were so anxious to be engaged, that they did not notice him, but while in this dangerous vicinity Fred saw one of his own men struggling to free himself from his fallen horse, to dismount and disentangle the man from the dead animal was the work of a moment, to get him up behind on his own good horse; was the work of another, but they had not gone far before they met two Affghans returning from the pursuit; these, expecting an easy victory, at once attacked them. One man attempted to cut the bridle, but it was a chain one, which entangled his sword for a moment, giving Fred an opportunity of cutting clean through his strong right arm; the other man aimed a savage blow at Fred's head, but the falling weapon only scratched the face, as he fell, shot through the heart by the trooper.

There was much rejoicing and great applause when Fred and the trooper rode into camp, and when the men heard their comrade's tale, they looked upon their dearly loved officer as if he was a divinity.

Marches, little fights, and great alarms, had passed away; Ghuzni had been stormed, Candahar had been taken, and occupied for many weary months with fears and strong forebodings that not a man would return to Hindoostan. Yet they did return with little loss, first witnessing the uncalled for and revengeful destruction of the Cabul Bazaar; then the bleaching bones of our unpractised commanders of our deluded army, and the unthought of though numerous followers in the dark, dismal defile of the Khyber; there were deep groans and deeper vows from Sepoys, Sowars, and Lascars, that they would never be seen there again.

The broken walls of Jellalabad, with the heroic memories of Sale and his comrades were left behind, and many a heart leaped with joy as the narrow passes of the grey mountains expanded into the valleys and plains of the Punjaub.

The hostile land was left behind, but memories of bitter things remained; there were hardships and losses of beloved comrades, and dire defeat; the Mahomedan felt that he had been fighting against his own creed—a thing forbidden; our own regiment of cavalry had sad memories—they had left many behind them with unmarked graves, but every officer and man remaining knew that they had done their duty, and now as they marched homewards, with many a weary mile to go, a strange duty was imposed upon them.

The vain glory of our Governor-General required a trophy, a symbol of victory where victory was not, but an escape was, and he selected for that purpose the old gates of the long since celebrated temple of Somnath; they would, he fancied, gratify the Hindoos. Did he think they would disgust the Mahomedans? He had captured them from the strongest citadel in Affghanistan, and they were fitting trophies to restore to the Hindoos.

Strange histories those old gates could tell, cut and fashioned by cunning carpenters, of strange device, and heavy beam. They had, in years gone by, witnessed the pious congregations of Hindoo devotees, their long processions and rich offerings, which, with excited crowds, had poured through their open, portals to the shrine of Somnath.

Then they had witnessed the hordes of conquering Mahomedans, in countless legions and with unbridled sway, pouring from the north with religion on the sword point, enforcing the outward sign of their own strong faith, and deluging the cities with torrents of dark red blood, from unoffending human beings; fanaticism and extermination were hand in hand. The Hindoo temples were destroyed, and these wondrous gates, of the holiest shrine of Western India were carried away by the Mahomedans as religious trophies, to the far famed fortress of Ghusni.

They could tell of the ribald jests of the Moslem host, of the insults they endured during their long weary march, of the danger they underwent of sharing the fate of their burnt fathers, and of the ignominy they felt at the remarks of those who assembled to witness their triumphant arrival.

They could tell of the perpetual troubles that shook the regions of central Asia, of fierce and unrelenting contests, of brave fights and treacherous murders, of brothers less forgiving than strangers, more cruel than the savage beasts of the jungles.

And now these patched up, battered gates were plucked away from the proud Mahomedan by a Christian, whose creed dictated charity to all, to whom a warlike trophy might be considered as a glory, to whom a religious trophy was a sad disgrace. Why should he tread on the faith of the millions who owned his sway, by taking from them, and restoring to Hindoos, a forgotten portion of a once sacred fane.

The deed was done, and these old logs of wood were on their road back to Somnath, to hang upon hinges which no longer existed. The Mussulmen were disgusted, the Hindoos smiled, and the fort of Agra was reached.

Then these gates could tell, if anything there is to tell, why they got no further; why the order of their triumphant march was not continued; and why to this day they still remain rotting, and uncared for in some dark corner of the Agra Fort.

The insult was already inflicted on the Mahomedan, and now a slight was put upon the Hindoo.

CHAPTER IX.

YUSUFF AND HOOSSEIN MEET AGAIN.

YUSUFF, the Hadji, sought all over Calcutta, without success, for Hoossein, on the morning after the departure of the emigrant coolie.

Calcutta was a large place; everyone in it was busy about his own affairs. Yusuff could find no one to search with him, to give him any information, or even to sympathise in his loss, which indeed appeared to be a very common one, and the insatiable Ganges invariably bore the blame.

Chotee Ma was inconsolable; she would not be persuaded that her son was possibly alive; she knew better—he was washed away in those turbid corpse laden waters, so she lighted her little oil light, on a fragment of cocoa-nut shell, and sending it adrift on the waters, waited a whole week on the Ghaut, in the fond hope that the little flickering lamp would guide her only son back again to his widowed mother. He came not, but despair did. She could never see him more on earth, and she prayed earnestly to go to Paradise. The river fogs, the pestilential exhalations, and scanty food fulfilled her wishes, and she died within a fortnight of her son's departure.

As Yusuff had visited Calcutta for the sole benefit of the young man, at the earnest solicitation of the widow, with the intention of helping the son of the friend who saved his life into some good situation, there was now no further occasion for his staying there.

The good old man was quite unhappy at

the melancholy result of his labours; he knew that a large circle of relations bewailed the troubles that had clouded the young man's existence, and he earnestly hoped to have been able to give them a satisfactory account of his progress. A night's lodging, a burra khana, depended on it, in more places than one; he had a thousand miles to travel by himself, and no good news to tell. There would be no dinners for the unwelcome guest.

It turned out, however, that his intelligence was received without regret. Hoossein was gone—it was his kismut; so the Hadji slept, and eat all the food that was given to him, much the same as usual, till he reached the end of his journey, the old Peer, at Roza.

To tell the truth, Yusuff had made the last few journeys with a slow foot and heavy heart. He rather dreaded the reception he should meet with, and the effect of the news on his fair daughter, Ameena. He knew that certain arrangements had been made for the marriage; the event depended much on the news he brought back. Fatima had quite made up her mind that Calcutta would soon put all former mistakes to rights; that the young man would find no evil associates there; in short, that the climate would do him as much good as a change of air benefits a sick person, and she whispered to her Hadji, as he departed,

"It is very desirable, for more reasons than one, that the marriage should take place soon."

With all this on his mind, Yusuff was astonished and rather hurt to find his news taken calmly; Fatima expressed no grief, and as for the girl she had almost forgotten him. Young people do forget soon! Some years had passed since they met; she only thought of him as her future husband, in compliance with the wishes of her parents.

"To be sure," said Ameena, "he was a very fine young man, a very promising fellow; but there were many more left."

The Hadji was more astonished, when he saw the reception given to a fine, good looking young man, Ibrahim, who walked into their abode as if he felt at home there.

The antecedents of Ibrahim were not very satisfactory; he had been for some time in rather suspicious service at Aurungabad; he had the reputation of beating the tom-tom beautifully, with the correct shrug of his shoulders, and expression of face, to be a capital master of ceremonies on natch nights; but at present he was a water carrier (bheestie), attached to the cavalry regiment stationed at ———. He was now on leave; there was no impediment to the marriage on his part, and as Hoossein was dead, there could now be none on the part of the lady.

Circumstances brought about the ceremony rather quicker than was intended; Ibrahim received orders to join, as his regiment was under marching orders. Great battles were expected, and all hands ordered to join immediately.

Fatima was naturally very unhappy, at the idea of losing her only comfort, and the more so as fighting was expected; but she consoled herself by remembering that her husband had once seen warfare, that she was by his side, that she cooked his daily bread; and as Ameena was actually born in regimental lines—why, she was used to it.

The marriage was duly solemnised with all the usual Mahomedan ostentation, and Ibrahim having placed his mussuchs (water bags) on his bullock, slinging a few household utensils over the hump, his bed, and his young laughing wife on the top of all, trudged merrily away to camp.

It was now about that period, when paddle wheels disturbed the placid wave of the Indian Ocean, when the overland route, through Egypt, was accomplished in litters, or chairs carried by two donkeys, by riding on them, or on camels, and the well known cart, drawn by four unbroken, runaway horses; only as they ran to the next stage and there stopped, the coachman always asked for his backsish with a satisfied smile.

These facilities in the journey between England and India induced great men to consider a short banishment, with a full purse, rather better that the ups and downs of old England with an empty one. The responsibility of an empire in the East was not considered very onerous, and the speech on taking leave of the East Indian Directors was an after-dinner one.

There had been, for long years, a normal occupation to be gone through in the East, a gorgeous ceremony, leading captive the Governors-General, forcing them, at times against their will, to fight with Peshwas, Rajahs, Maha-Majahs, and all the hosts of rulers over provinces contiguous to their own, to which the said provinces were in due time annexed.

Of course, by this process, our empire became very large and very valuable, so that, when rumour brought the intelligence that the

Russians were tampering with our warlike northern neighbours, with the intention of invading this empire, it was very natural for our Governor-General to turn the tables, and invade them, either with a view of coercing the men beyond the mountains into an alliance with us, or coaxing into friendship men who had never been friends.

We have seen in the last chapter the unhappy results of some of these gorgeous ceremonies. It was the fate of India never to remain quiet.

There was an old prophecy, that when the English crossed the Indus in arms, they would lose Hindostan. The rumour was talked of everywhere. The Punjaub heard of it. The Kalsa army, drilled by Europeans, well armed, brave men, the bequest of Runjeet Sing, talked of it. They had seen our defeat in the Khyber; they had witnessed our distress, and had given us their protection. Our friend, the old Lion of the Punjaub, had gone, so the Kalsa army determined to win some glory for itself. In strong hope, confident of victory, their great host crossed the Sutlej river, and invaded the English empire in the year 1845.

Yusuff found himself entangled in the warfare that followed; he was a sutler, but disguised it under the name of merchant. He supplied the wants of the Mussulman soldiers in the British camp, buying and picking up articles found on the battle fields. There were golden-hilted swords, jewelled pistols, ivory-handled daggers, and inlaid matchlocks. The fights of Moodkee and Ferozeshah had supplied a goodly load. It was a very exciting time. The old man said it made him young again—yet he always expected to be robbed and murdered. No one was more punctual on the field of battle. If there was carnage, he was in it almost before the strife had ceased. He was considered a dexterous hand at collecting valuables from the dead; and if a wounded man attempted resistance, there was something at hand to keep him quiet.

The Hadji was busy in his vocation on the evening of the 10th of February, 1846. The Sikhs, dislodged from their entrenchments at Sobraon, their guns taken, and their whole army in confusion, were endeavouring to cross the Sutlej by their bridge of boats. Yusuff was led on by the rapidity of the pursuit, till he reached the banks overlooking the river; there he was picking up valuables, quicker than usual, intently occupied, when he was saluted by a slap on the back, and an exclamation of " Shah-bas, Hadji Saheb!"

There was no time for explanation. Yusuff was in much consternation at the unexpected meeting. Visions of discord sprang up before him—anticipations of he scarcely knew what came over him. But at that instant the British artillery crowned the bank beside them.

Unsparing, never missing, the deadly weapons sent their grape-shot, in rattling volleys, amidst the confused mass of the Sikh soldiers as they struggled and fought among themselves for the narrow passage of the reeling bridge over that terrible river, across which they had passed in hope and exultation only a few months before. They hoped it would protect them now. Vain hope! Masses on masses crowded on; masses on masses rolled over. The shaking platform was a trap and a snare. No shot missed their entangled numbers; the very planks were broken, and they tumbled through—the dead, the wounded, and the living, formed one heaving, conglomerated mass. Weaker and weaker became the swaying bridge, as chain and rope were shot away, till at last the swinging fabric gave way in several places. The hindmost men perceived it not, but still pressing on, in frightened and unheeding haste, drove their comrades into the surging wave, and followed themselves, until there was a thick, writhing mass of drowning men.

Uprose from that shattered host a wailing cry, loud and long. Close to Yusuff's ear there sounded a rattling laugh—at that moment a strange and unwelcome sound. The scene was too dreadful for laughter, thought the Hadji, as he turned round to rebuke the levity, and there, close beside him, sitting on his heels, with his elbows on his knees, his chin on his fists, was the face of the long lost Hoossein, gloating over the slaughter and destruction in that fatal river.

"It will all go to the bottom! Shitan will get it all," were the words he uttered, as the firing ceased. "We shall never find anything." While they still contemplated the scene, the lurid sun vanished, the day was done, and the two found their way back to Yusuff's tent.

To the inquiries of the latter, where he had come from? how long he had come? had he been dead? and many other questions, Hoossein replied that "he had come from the other end of the world." He had been up in time to see the Sikhs cross in their glory, and a few of them go back in despair. "I was," he said, "in hopes that they would have stood. I did all I could to help them. Our cavalry attended to my wishes, and would not charge; but that cursed artillery of the English has been the ruin of the thing. If it had not been for that, they would have been eaten up, driven into the sea, and—" Hoossein made a significant gesture with both hands round his neck.

"You see, Hadji Sahib," he continued, "I hate the English. I came away from Jamaica because they told me I should be hanged if I staid. The fact was a great many rich coolies died in my house. I could not help their getting ill and coming there to rest. It was no fault of mine that they died. What they left behind them was not enough to pay for their funeral expenses. However, I thought it best to be on the safe side, so got stowed away in a ship as a bit of cargo, and came to Calcutta. There was no one there, no business to be done, so I came on here, where it seems lively enough. I have got my little tent with the cavalry, so good night, Hadji Sahib; we shall meet again."

The old man, for various reasons, did not wish to see Hoossein again, so the next morning he packed up his goods, and went away.

Quick of eye, dexterous of hand, cruel and determined, Hoossein rapidly accumulated so much, that he set up shop for himself. He pitched a handsome tent; he placed neat divans around it; he entertained musicians and Natch girls. He had picked up some refinements in the West, which he adapted to Oriental tastes, and his tent soon became the favourite resort for the idle Mahomedan troopers of the army.

In the meantime there was but little rest while a man of the enemy remained under arms. The army pressed on to Lahore; that noble old soldier, Sir Robert Sale, died of his wounds, content to go to his rest, with his untarnished sword beside him.

Victorious and successful, a treaty of peace was signed. The Governor-General and the

Commander-in-Chief were honoured by their Sovereign with the peerage, and thanked by the Parliament of England, and the East India Company.

History will some day find out that the rewards were small for winning so heavy a stake.

CHAPTER X.

HOOSSEIN SWIMS AGAINST THE STREAM.

HOOSSEIN pitched his tent near the mausoleum of the great conqueror Jehanjire. He bought and sold without any reverence for that beautiful building, for its sacred inscriptions, its elegant mosaics, or its overpowering reminiscences; it was a fine place for the exercise of his abilities. There was a grand mixture of young men in and about Lahore, so that the talim khana, established by Hoossein, in one of the courts of the tomb, was the resort of the highest native officers of the Anglo-Indian army.

The Natch girls, the new inventions—those happy mixtures of opium, of tobacco, of spirits, under names which did not outrage the feelings of the strictest Mahomedans, yet had the effect of introducing indulgers to a temporary sojourn outside the gates of Paradise. The wrestlers, the jugglers, and the card-playing, filled the dimly-lighted divan nightly to overflowing.

Hoossein felt he was going on very well, but having consulted his high priest, or the high priest having intimated to him that he ought to enter into the bonds of matrimony, he informed the venerable Moolah, under a promise of secresy, that he was already betrothed, but knew not where the lady was to be found.

The Moolah enjoined the strictest search, the most minute enquiry, and engaged, if it could be proved that the girl was dead, or otherwise disposed of, that Hoossein should be absolved from his vows, and be at liberty to make fresh ones.

Under this arrangement, Hoossein began to live merrily; he became intimate with several Sikh gentlemen, who had seen something of the world, and profited by their wanderings; who quite understood Hoossein's aspirations, and desired to help them on for the benefit of their own nation in general, and themselves in particular. They entered into all his feelings against the English; they were fully aware that what he said was true, that they had been too hasty, and had not kept sufficient reserves in hand, and, as night after night they chatted over the situation, they began to see a light in the horizon.

The Earl of Dalhousie, "*ora et Labora*," had assumed the reins of India with a firm hand. Nothing was to be left in doubt by him; so as the distant region of Mooltan seemed in that condition, and as policy required a safe, high road in that direction, it was resolved to clear it up.

Two promising young men, Mr. Vans Agnew, and Lieutenant Anderson, were ordered off to Mooltan, with small escort, to ascertain precisely the feelings of the Dewan Moolraj towards the Government of India.

It was so arranged by the Sikh gentlemen and Hoossein, that a friend of theirs should accompany this party. It reached Mooltan in safety; the ambassadors had an interview with Moolraj, and then they were ruthlessly and cruelly slaughtered, upholding in their last sad moments, the truth, dignity, and bravery of their country.

This murder of peaceful ambassadors was the cause of a renewal of the war in a distant country, far away from the usual resources of the Indian Government, against an enemy who knew that his last hope of independance was in the scale. The second Sikh war proved—if proof were wanting—that no orientals, however well led, however determined, and however numerous, could hold their own against the determined courage and the magnificent discipline of the English army.

To return to Mooltan : it so happened that an Englishman turned up unexpectedly, but very opportunely. There was no army, no money, no stores, no arms, no ammunition, within many hundred miles; yet there was one Englishman, not far off, in civil charge of a province, and he took on himself the extraordinary task of avenging the cold-blooded murder.

This hero, Lieutenant Edwardes, collected money, supplies, and men; he made, or he found ammunition ; he expended a great many English promises (promises never broken), and in two months time, this solitary officer engaged, and defeated the forces of Moolraj, drove them into Mooltan, and kept them there.

What was so far accomplished by this undrilled and badly supplied force, could not be finished by a General at the head of a large army from Bengal ; the Dewan or his fortress could not be captured; the Sepoys refused to work in the trenches (every man should have been buried in them); and the General had to raise the siege, till a Bombay army, unaffected with the secret springs of evil, enabled him to begin again, and to take the place.

On what chances the fate of kingdoms depend! Had it not been for Edwardes, the whole of the Mooltan army would have been at liberty to join Shere Shing, who, like the hydra sprung up again to fight. On the 22nd of November, 1848, he had forty thousand men, and twenty-eight guns, and was beaten at Rannuggur. On the 13th January, 1849, he was beaten at Chillianwallah, with great loss, and suffered severely in several smaller engagements. Yet on the 21st of February, his army had increased to sixty thousand men, with fifty-nine guns—so ready were the men of this country to rally for the fight round the standard of their race.

When Hoossein found that a Bombay force

had come to the rescue at Mooltan, he immediately left that place, with the expression,

"I never liked the Mahrattas."

When the Sikh force was utterly discomfited at Goojerat, he was at one time in great danger of being cut off with an unfulfilled destiny. He was, it is true, pretty well in the rear of the army; but though he knew the Sikhs could run well, he never expected a pursuit to continue, as it did, for fifteen or twenty miles; he, his Natch girls, and fiddlers, were enveloped in the crowd; the British sabre swung unsparingly. There was William Havelock to be avenged, but it was spared from shedding such blood as that of Hoossein's.

Hoossein's arrow had missed its aim. He had fondly hoped that the Sikhs would drive the English into the sea; he began to doubt if all that Sambo had told him, was true. Sambo never saw an army of twenty-five thousand men, commanded by an English

Lord Saheb, beat an army of sixty thousand good and very brave soldiers. Sambo must have seen some bad specimens, or Sambo must have told lies. At any rate, the British army had persevered; it had fought through great difficulties to the end; and the Sikh army surrendered unconditionally. The vast kingdom of the Punjab was annexed to the British Empire in the east. Lord Gough had gone home in triumph, Sir Charles Napier had succeeded him as Commander-in-Chief of the Indian army, and with no one left to make war with on the Indian Peninsula, the horizon appeared, to casual observers, as one of peace, civilisation, and prosperity.

When all was settling down into the usual routine of camp life, an accidental meeting with a trooper roused the dormant venom in Hoossein's heart.

The army was at rest; there was no foe; men got leave. Delhi, the abode of Hoossein for the present, was also the home of a great many men of the Indian army. The divans filled well. Yusuff was there, and had explained all about Ameena's marriage, expressing his surprise at never hearing anything about her, when one evening, as Hoossein was recounting his adventures with the Hadji near him, a stranger happened to mention the —— regiment of cavalry. Yusuff immediately asked after his son-in-law, Ibrahim.

"Ah!" said the trooper; "Ibrahim, our bheestie, he was soon gone; he was not strong enough to hold so fair a prize as the lottery of life had given him. He was washed off, far away, and never came back to tell the truth; cunning hands, nearly as safe as Thugs,"—Hoossein turned to listen—"did that business, only they kept the houri. It is rumoured that she has been seen in the tent of the Sahib Lōg."

"Is that true?" asked Hoossein.

"I was told so by one I believed," replied the man.

"Did you say Ibrahim was drowned?

Who drowned him?" enquired Hoossein, sharply.

"How should I know?" was the reply. "I only tell you what I heard from another. The Sahib's name I heard was Eglington Sahib. If you want to know more you had better go to ——, and find out for yourself. One would think, by the manner of your asking, that you have an interest in the subject."

Hoossein was silent for a moment; a sudden light seemed to gleam upon him.

"Yes," he said; "these are the stings we bear in silence, and have borne for years, but at last the venom spreads over the system, like the poison of the cobra"—he hesitated for a moment, as the memory of his nativity sprung up like a phantom before him,—" till the whole body becomes dormant, insensible to its suffering, and dies out like the lamp without its oil. So shall we die, my friends; burden after burden is placed upon us, we are covered with ignominy, the castes of the

Hindoos are laughed at, the religion of the Mahomedan is scorned, our women are defiled, and all of us are called niggers.

" The English have now no more enemies; they will devote their time to trample on us. Look around, see how they drive the poor ignorant cultivators into the bonds of slavery. They have forbidden suttee to the Brahmins, the Rajpoots can no longer destroy their new born daughters. Is this their love to them? or is it love to the women ? They are innovations on your rights, and a destruction of your ceremonies. Look to it! consider the gates of Somnath ; look at the indignity and insult! Our bread has been defiled by the Caffir.

" It is my advice to all. I call it out here, and on the house top, in my early prayer, and when I repeat my neemaz at the sunset. Stick up for your religious rites, for your caste privileges; let not the slightest tittle escape you. If you give in on one point, you may as well give in on all ; if we do not determine to hold together we may as well say so. We shall then know that we have no common cause, that we are no longer brethren in affliction. We have won an empire for the Englishman, with the sweat of our bodies and the blood of our hearts. We, a vast multitude, powerful and courageous, are yet afraid to blot out our oppressors from the land.

"My friends," continued Hoossein, in his low lisping notes, "if we do not drive them into the sea, they will take our women and destroy our religions."

The speech was received with some sensation; no one replied to it at once; but the company fell into little knots, talking amongst themselves.

After a time an old Soubadar, while quietly smoking his callioon, said,

"Hoossein Sahib, I have been thinking over what you said just now. You talk of driving the English into the sea; I was quite a young man in 1803, in the service of the

Rajah of Berar. My master and Scindiah Maharajah thought as you do, they threatened to drive the English into the sea. My father was a brave man; I stood at his side at the head of his regiment. He told me it was as easy to curb the ocean as to stop the Topee Wallahs, as they marched on to the attack at Assaye; and so it proved, for they utterly routed ten times their number.

"I shall never forget that evening, as we sat on the banks of a stream with no supper to eat, with the lamentations of the wounded ringing in our ears. How my father talked to me and one or two others. 'It is of no use,' he said, 'fighting against these Gora Lōg.' Suraj Dowlah put one hundred and fifty of them into a cage, where ten men would have died in a night; and behold, when the morning came, there were fifty of them still living. After that, he, with an army of fifty thousand men, was beaten by Clive Saheb with three thousand. Could all this have happened if it had not been destiny?

"My father went on to tell us that the white man was just and true, that he never took needless revenge, as the Mahomedan King of Persia had done at Delhi, when an indiscriminate massacre was ordered, and continued till his weary soldiers walked knee deep in human blood; when one hundred and fifty thousand men, women, and children were known to have perished; and thousands more were never heard of, who had trusted the clemency of the wild beast of the jungle in preference to the unrelenting fury of man. All this was done under pretence of Mahomedan sanctity.

"It is true that the English fight and kill all they can by fair means; but I myself have seen a white soldier aiding a wounded enemy. I have been with them ever since the battle I told you of. I have risen from a Sepoy to be an officer. From youth nearly to the end of natural life"—here the old man curled his thin white moustache—" but have never seen any intention amongst them of taking our women, or abusing our religions.

"I have brothers and relations who cultivate the white man's land. In former times they lived in villages with high walls and lofty turrets, on which the watchmen stood to give warning of marauders; the towers and the walls are now in ruins, the goats and the cattle feed upon their sites, and the watchmen are not wanted. There is but little robbery, the taxes are light, there is security for life, and we can now get rich without the fear of being plundered by our rulers. Even in my own time, under the Mahratta or the Mahomedan rule, you, Hoossein Saheb, would have had to pay your way, while now you escape all taxation.

"There is more than this; they educate us, they make roads for us, they give us employment, and pay honestly for work done. I have seen some and heard of other great works, of former days, where Mussulman kings and Mahratta chiefs sat by, and saw their subjects working till they died, and their unpaid corpses were buried beneath the works they helped to raise. The English do not do these things. Do you, Hoossein Saheb, wish to bring us back to such doings?

"The English are here as our conquerors. In my poor opinion, they act with wisdom and moderation, compared with those I have known. They rule us with justice and with mercy. Would any of us do so, if destiny placed us in their position?"

The Soubadar had smoked quietly till he came to the last few words, when some strong whiffs finished his callioon and the conversation.

CHAPTER XI.

MAHOMEDANS AND MAHRATTAS.

HOOSSEIN could not rest. His conscience was uneasy. Yet did he seize every opportunity of scattering his venom. For many months he met with small success. The remembrance of the late actions were fresh; there was extra pay unspent; some plunder to consume, and a weariness of labour enjoying itself in rest.

There was an eagle's eye at the head of the army. *Regarde bien,* his wings were closed, but ready to open and pounce on any fitting quarry. He knew full well that there was a feeling of discontent abroad. He had marked the regiments which had refused their duty; he had watched, with careful attention, the little demands, the last complaints and unreasonable petitions; he had marked, with sorrow, the growing inclination to give all that was asked for; he had, of all others, attended carefully to the real wants of the soldier, and omitted nothing, in reason, tending to their comfort and convenience.

But this care had a limit. His wings were kept closed, as they longed to flutter in kindness over his army. He was restrained by the Governor-General from doing what he considered right and just, and sooner than stay at the head of the soldiers whom he could not rule as he wished, he gave up his magnificent command, with a warning that the Bengal Sepoy should be carefully watched.

Rest and indulgence, idleness and discontent, followed fast in each other's footsteps.

The finest figured soldier in the world began again to grumble at nothing.

There was an unclean thing in his path—the shadow of an unbeliever in Krishna fell upon his bread—he had not sufficient time for his poojah—Christians had more privileges than Brahmins—and English officers laboured to convert Hindoos from the faith of their fathers.

When they found these trivial things attended to, complaints became more frequent, rights were demanded as if from equals, obedience to orders and the performance of duty depended on the Sepoy's pleasure, and several regiments had been pronounced in a state of insubordination.

Hoossein began to travel about rapidly. He visited Lahore, Agra, Meerut, Lucknow, Barrackpoor, Cawnpore, and many other large camps. He inserted his poison fang in all, and in all found many followers, eager and anxious for the fray. He discovered that there was no vanity in the world equal to that of the Purdasee Sepoy; and while working on that vanity, he hoped to make it instrumental to the advancement of the Mahomedans.

With these he plotted carefully. No act of theirs was to bring down suspicion upon them. He even found fault with them for their too open hatred to the English in the Sikh war. They were to be the most humble and obsequious soldiers of the state, and Hoossein was delighted to find that the Mussulman trooper was a very careful and considerate man.

Often at this time did the conversations of Sambo recur to his memory. "How is it," he said one day, "that you soldiers, for many generations, are afraid to do what the African, who is not a soldier, will not hesitate to perform?"

"It is just that which makes the difference," said a Sepoy. "The negro does not know the danger he incurs. We do."

"Then," retorted Hoossein, "you confess you are afraid."

"The tiger and the cobra are not afraid," replied the young man, "but wait the opportunity. The negro is like the timid antelope, which attacks the wolf as it springs upon her fawn."

"And dies," said the other.

"Not always," replied the Sepoy; "their rashness sometimes carries them clear."

"But," said Hoossein, "the negro is not timid in all things. He has no hesitation in shedding blood; he rather delights in it. On occasion he will stab the paramour of his wife, and walk to the gallows, glorying in the deed. Yet it is difficult to induce him to ride a horse." There was a laugh. "We can do the latter, yet not the former. If blood is to be shed, you are content to shed it by cutting off the noses of the women."

"And serve them right," was the reply. "If we cannot get justice done us, of course we take the vengeance on ourselves."

"Why cannot you get justice?" cried Hoossein; "I can tell you — because the judges are bribed, or share in the crime. There is nothing done without money."

"That is very true," remarked another. "I recollect once, many years ago, when I was with the Pulton at Salapoor, we Sepoys got into a row with the citizens, about the women. The police joined against us; but we had some good latees, and licked them well. The case came before a young Sahib, who, to tell the truth, was anxious to do justice; but we got up a little purse in the Pulton, bribed witnesses, clerks, and police, so that no one could tell, for a certainty, whether there had or had not been a fight."

"There was a talk the other day," said a young cavalry Naique, "that in Western India, a great man, hand in hand with the Lord Sahib, big wigs, and great ladies, is bought up by the people to interfere with judges, magistrates, and police, and that as it was becoming notorious, an inquiry was to be made into this almost undisguised Khut-Put."

"We had better remedy this state of things," said Hoossein. "Let us turn out those who will not give justice to the people. Let us exterminate them, and make Dewanees and Foujdarees, where justice will be administered without bribery and without favour. We will issue our zairnamahs, that all who wish for justice shall come to—" Hoossein paused.

"Hoossein Ben Hassan, the mirror of justice," cried a man, laughing, "He will be the only one of us who objects to receive value for his work. A very honest man, who lives on the welfare of his neighbours without their knowing it; who takes the honey from the flower, but robs it of no sweetness; who drinks the water from the chattie, yet always leaves it full; whose buttie does not burn its oil; and whose impartiality cannot distinguish the beggar from the king."

"Hoossein Ben Hassan, the picture of Insaf, shall be our judge," cried another. "He has seen a great deal of the world, and learned something from that clever fellow, the African. No one knows better than Hoossein, when our rulers do wrong. It seems to be pretty often. As we cannot correct each individual, it will be as well to take Hoossein's advice, and exterminate them. But they are scattered all over the country, and how are we to get at them. I once heard a reciter tell a tale of some big monster with a hundred heads—a dangerous and a savage beast; but he was to be killed. So they cut, and they burned, and they strangled, and shot, and pounded, and sliced; but there were always heads left. So will it be now, if we don't look out,—and heads with sharp teeth in them."

"Who cares for the teeth?" said Hoossein, "they can do no harm against numbers; we can kill this one as they did the other beast; the Bengal army is strong enough to drive them into the sea; the Madras army could do the same; it is only the cringing Mahratta who prefer the chains of slavery."

"No!" cried a small, black, bright eyed man from a distant part of the room, and he stood erect on his wiry legs as he spoke. " The Mahratta does not cringe. We are a conquered race, and we eat the salt of our conquerors with content; we fight his battles and receive his pay; under other masters we never got the pay, though we did fight; we got no pensions, now we do; there is no forced labour, then there was; there was no prize money, now there is; if I found a bracelet on the battle field it was taken from me, now it is not; there are no murdering Thugs or Dacoits, then there were; there were ravishing Pindaries, there are none now; the collectors of revenue misapplied their collections, they do not do so now; the cultivators were always debtors to the state, they are not so now; they were plundered by Mussulmen and by Brahmin, the English take no more than their due; they give no leases, but never turn a man out of his field, as long as he pays his land tax."

"Stop!" cried a well-dressed man, in a white, long-cloth angrica, a fine cotton turban on his head, cotton gloves on his hands, and cotton stockings on his feet. "You are an indolent race. You will not work unless you are obliged to do so, and the more you are called on to pay, the more you will exert yourselves."

"The tyrants of olden days," replied the Mahratta, "found that out; they discovered that when they had ground us down to the bone, we could neither work nor fight. Do you think that the English could have conquered our empire if the people had been taught to love, and not to hate their rulers. I speak of all, Mussulman, Rajpoot, Sikh, and Brahmin, they all plundered the people—the company Sirkar does not; may they meet with their reward! The Zemindar," he continued, "speaks of his own people, whom he understands. The Mahrattas are not an idle race; the Coonbees are good men and true, and very thankful that they are not under the Zemindary system, where labour and property have been appropriated by the landholder; and, as far as my poor senses can see, I think it is better policy for a Government to have thousands of good wills, than the sole good will of a Zemindar; it is true that his cultivators would possibly follow his opinion, but you must allow that one man is more likely to be influenced by caprice than a thousand, each one of whom had an interest in the soil he tills, and the Sirkar that protects him."

"See how we have been protected; there are many of us Merasdars, who have held the same property from the Peishwas, to the English rule; it is our own and held sacred; what native government would have done this?"

"Ah!" said the Zemindar, " those Merasdars, of whom you speak, are now in course of disinheritance by the Enam commission; they had, it appears, in many instances, no real claim on their possessions; there must be a great cry against a government for treating occupants so shamefully."

"You mistake the case," replied the Mahratta; "not a single Merasdar has been turned out of his Meras tenure; they are Enamdars whom you allude to, and many of them may thank their stars that they enjoyed their estates so long, when they had no title to them. Formerly there was a court of Serdars in the Deccan, to attend to the affairs of the nobles, but that court could not, or did not look into anything, unless it was brought formally to its notice; it was no one's business to report lapse of service or failures of lineal descent; indeed, it was more likely to have been the interest of many not to mention such things.

"In course of time, discord, family disputes, and native jealousy, brought hidden things to light. The Enam commission was appointed, and has resumed many properties illegally enjoyed. Some of these people may have been Merasdars; if so, they enjoy those rights still."

"But," said the Zemindar, "your money is all taken from you, and never spent in the country. Mine is all spent on the spot."

"What comes to your share may be," was the reply; "but with many Zemindars that is not the case. Some of them never go near the estates, unless to collect the revenue, and as much more as they can find, and spend their share in very irregular living elsewhere. Of late years, the spare money which the wars have left, has been expended on roads, bridges, tanks, and aqueducts, so that the money, or some of it, which we pay as revenue comes back for our benefit."

"Are you not all in debt?" was then asked, "and are you not all slaves to your money lenders?"

"We are a careless race," the Mahratta answered; "but I believe that there are many in the world worse off than we are. We like to see our sons make a good start in life, and we do not curtail the wedding expenditure; we should be bad Hindoos if we did. The Shroffs tease and annoy us, but we are not slaves to them. We cannot blame the authorities on these accounts, and there is no cause of anger between us."

"I believe," said Hoossien, "that although you are a soldier, you are a coward, Gunnoo Saheb; that you only speak up for your Sirkar, because you are afraid of evil consequences."

The jet black eyes of Gunnoo flashed like living balls of fire for a moment; then in the same calm voice, he said,

"History will tell the Mahomedan that the Mahratta is no coward ; you yourself, Hoossein Saheb, have seen our Pultuns march up to the guns which Bengal Sepoys refused to take; you have seen us scramble up the breach which the Bengal Sepoy had recoiled from. As for myself, I would not wish this assembly to think that I am a coward;

I am small, and the men around are large, but I am willing to try a fall in your talim khana with any man you please to bring; I will do my best!"

"Sha-Bass, Gunnoo!" was loudly repeated through the room, as the now excited company rose from their seats, and repaired to the talim khana.

CHAPTER XII.

FASHION.

THE talim khana, into which the young men retired, was a spacious shed, with raised terraces all round for the spectators to sit upon; there was an oblong excavation in the centre, about twenty feet long, by sixteen feet wide. The shed was dimly lighted up by several oil lights, suspended from the roof, hanging over the pit.

The lamps shone on two fine young men, having a trial of strength for their own amusement. As soon as one of them was thrown, the saw dust in the pit was raked level, some fresh dust was thrown down, and the place was declared ready for the struggle of the evening.

The company quietly seated themselves, in full expectation of seeing Gunno exterminated by Persaud Sing, the young mañ selected for the occasion by Hoossein, out of many aspirants to the honour.

Bets, as long as the purses, were offered on the Bengali, with no takers, one unknown individual only accepting, as a favour, a few of the long odds.

Persaud Sing stepped into the arena first, with a smile of anticipated victory; he salamed to the spectators, as he stood in the centre of the pit to be looked over.

He was a fine young man, in fair condition, slightly too fleshy for hard work; he was about twenty-five years of age; rather more than six feet high; with great breadth of shoulders, a fine tapering waist, rather slack about the loins, with powerful hips and thighs, but deficient in his legs. No one could look upon his long powerful arms without feeling that, once within their grasp there would be no escape.

Persaud Sing was, indeed, the most powerful wrestler the cantonment could boast of; he had been known to hurl his opponents from one end of the arena to the other; in fact, he had disabled so many of his comrades, that they had been forbidden to wrestle with him in earnest. Strangers were not included in the colonel's orders.

When Gunnoo sprang into the ring, and made his obeisance to the company, there was a general inclination to smile. He did not reach to the shoulders of his opponent, but as he walked round with a grave and undisturbed countenance, with a firm step, and dauntless air, the spectators could not but admire his sinewy figure; he was about twenty-eight years of age, in the full vigour of manhood; his head was small, and remarkably round, sitting with singular ease on a muscular neck, falling off with a beautiful slope to strong shoulders, and wiry arms; his chest was full and broad, covered with thick, curly hair; his loins and hips were finely developed, running down into enormous thighs, with little short knees, and calves full of sinew, but rather ungainly in shape, finishing off with ugly feet; the insteps were well arched, but there was an undue extension of the heel, with a spreading of the toes, not conducive to beauty. He excited much admiration, and some pity.

The two men were naked, with the exception of the cloth round their loins, and that was rolled into a strong, tight band.

Hoossein gave the signal to begin.

The opponents stood fronting one another; both now salamed, and touching each other's hands, they smacked their bent arms, and the hollows of their thighs, eyeing each other intently, while withdrawing to a little distance.

Persaud, smiling, walked towards Gunnoo,

with an easy, off-hand way, endeavouring to seize his waist. This was evaded, by a slight bound backwards; Gunnoo now, with his hands on his knees, with head bent forward, and eyes scanning every thought and motion of his adversary, kept moving backwards and forwards, or circling round. Persaud made many efforts to seize him, which were avoided with the greatest ease.

The Mahratta moved like a cat, the Bengali laboured hard to catch him; the excitement —great at first—began to calm down a little, as several minutes passed in these futile attempts to close.

The spectators cried out that both men were afraid.

Persaud renewed his efforts, but all were still evaded. Suddenly, Gunnoo sprang from one end back to the centre of the arena, and there, for the first time, stood erect, with both arms extended to the side, and his left foot a little advanced.

"Ho!" cried Persaud, as he sprang towards him, with his long arms, in the act of embracing him.

A bend of the body, a side inclination, and Gunnoo was inside of—but below—the young giant's arms, while his own grasped that slim waist.

Persaud was raised from the ground; Gunnoo made one small step forwards, and his foe, apparently without much effort, was tossed fairly over his right shoulder, with a tremendous crash, right into the centre of the pit.

"Wah! wah! Sha bas!" cried the astonished spectators.

"The Mahratta is not afraid," said Gunnoo, in his quiet, but clear voice, as he stooped to help up his antagonist.

There was a convulsive move of the hands of the large man, as he lay on the sawdust, as if clutching at some moving or unseen thing. There was a quivering of the legs, but the head laid back beneath the motionless shoulder.

"He is dead," cried one.

"Bring some vinegar," said another.

"It is of no use," said Hoossein, who had stepped into the pit, and raised the body. "He is dead! His neck is broken! I thought so."

No one ventured to dispute such an experienced opinion.

Gunnoo retired to clothe himself, and submit—as he was told he must—to a court of enquiry.

The dark stranger gathered up his bets, and the company, rising from their seats, returned to the divan, to talk over the very strange event.

"A capital pilewan, and an old hand," was generally allowed, till the betting man remarked that he was not a very old hand at it, neither was he considered very good.

A tall young fellow, laughing, said,

"Not a good one? Why, he must be, to kill our best man."

"We have a great many who can beat

Gunnoo," was the reply. " You thought your man good, because he had never been tried except among yourselves. If you go about the world a little, you will find your level; you flatter yourselves too much."

The circle was in no humour to hear further taunts; symptoms of irritation arose, and it might have become unpleasant to the stranger, who had just made so many enemies, when a white-haired old man, of fine bearing, cried out,

" Bus! silence!" and thus continued : " I have often told you the same, young men. You live alone, and you get all you ask for. You are let off half your duty, if you refuse to work, on the plea of religion or caste; your pleas are allowed. I do not see where it will all end; but this I do see, that you are an idle, dissipated lot; and if I live long enough, I shall see some of you Sepoys and troopers hung. As for you, Zemindars, you will go on skinning your slaves, and defrauding Government, till one or the other skin you.

You aspire to be kings now. I would advise you to remain quiet; your doings will not bear enquiry.

This old man was a privileged scold; he had been one of them, but was now a pensioner for wounds and distinguished services; his harangue caused much laughter. General smoking and general conversation ensued; the company broke up into small parties for coffee or card playing, and the evening relapsed into its usual routine.

A set of musicians came into the room with the inexpressible music of the East, then flowers were strewed upon the floor, a few garlands were distributed, some sandal-wood oil and attar of roses were sprinkled on garments and kerchiefs, while those who had been so honoured, rose to depart.

Those intending to remain now removed to one end of the room, and presently a set of Natch girls entered. Their tom-tom beat its dull monotonous sound, their sitars and geettars twanged their wiry strings, the women twisted, and turned, and wriggled, and moved about, tinkling their bracelets, their armlets, and anklets, in the most approved style.

There is an unaccountable fashion in every thing, and these three girls were now all the fashion at P——Poor. They were all ugly, one of them was growing wrinkles—these come very early in the East, Natch girls live very hard lives.

Ailee, the eldest, had never known any thing else but hardship; she had been sold as a child by her own mother in a time of famine, to keep herself and two younger daughters alive, but Ailee was ugly, so that her price only fed the rest of her family a few days, and then they all died. As she was cheap, she was not cared for, but placed on drudgery and menial occupations. She was sent out at night with the other girls to carry the lantern, and to hold the slippers, to punka her companions, when hot, and to drive off mosquitoes.

Some how or another no one ever thought

of Ailee except to scold her; she did not recollect ever doing any thing right in her juvenile years, except not to grow; she did not do it on purpose, but she thought it quite right, as she never had a kind word said to her except in reference to her size, "What a nice little girl," and then the frequenters of the house petted her because she was so small, and Ailee was at last coaxed to sing, and her voice was called a sweet little voice, and very like the little Bulbul; and then Ailee had been coaxed to dance—such dancing, enveloped in old muslin and embroidered garments, with a great ugly necklace, which hung very heavy on her little neck; so did the other ornaments hang very heavy on her delicate shoulders; but they were all fashionable, so she learned to wear them till she became fashionable herself, and gave the right swagger in the dance, and tuned up her notes just when the touching music of the soft tom-tom required it, and cast up her eyes just when people expected her to do so, and shook her bracelets and toe rings when the pleasant soft cymbals prevented any one hearing them, and advanced, and retired, and wriggled about in the most fashionable style of dancing girls; so it was not to be wondered at that in time Ailee came into fashion herself, and she was more in fashion this night than usual, for a good deal of excitement had been got up, and fresh people were still coming in to hear how the unfortunate termination of the wrestling match occurred; it was, in fact, a sensation night at Hoossein Sahib's divan, and it was very well known that little Ailee had very much patronised Persaud Sing; and there were many young men who would have been very glad to step into his slippers.

Persaud's pretty turban had been given to him by Ailee; she had a high character for liberality, in fact she was all the fashion, and it would have been very wrong for any one not to wish to be noticed by her. When she liked it she had many fascinating bewitching little ways, and she tried some of them with the betting stranger, flinging a necklace of Mogree flowers round his neck, and bringing her face very close to his while doing so; then she sidled towards him as she sang "The land of the stranger;" but he never even looked at her; he did not know that she was in fashion; so he was given up, and a little bouquet of jessamine was given to a young Hindoostan man, who accepted it with a very grateful smile, for he knew the value of it, and the fashion of the thing. So Ailee was pleased, and sang with vehemence, songs about "Heroes in War," and "Heroes in Love," which the tall young man put in his kumer bund, having no pocket, and volunteered to carry Ailee's lantern home for her, as it was a dark night; he hoped to get an invitation to supper, but he did not, and was left out in the cold and in the dark, with a streak of red glare from an upper window streaming across the street; and Ramdeen looked up to see where it came from, and saw an open lattice, with European soldiers sitting in it, and while he looked up, Ailee stepped up and talked to them, at which they appeared to be much pleased; but he was not, and vowed a great vow by all the worst inhabitants of Jehannum, that he never would speak to Ailee again; and he did not sleep sound that night by reason of the very hot people he invoked to carry Ailee away; but he was a good natured fellow, and got cool next morning, and was very glad after parade to get a glance from the wrinkled syren of fashion, with a pawn leaf, containing a little chunam and a little supare nut, which he chewed, and listened to Ailee while she abused the Europeans, and told him of a great many things which they had not done, but which he believed they had, and for the doing of which he hated them exceedingly, and went to consult Hoossein on the subject of immediate vengeance.

Hoossein gave him very good advice, begging him to do nothing of the sort in a hurry, and repent of it at leisure, but if he had a grievance (he would he a rare mortal if he had not), he should consider how to square accounts with the greatest possible convenience to himself; he also advised him not to call on so many of the old people of the Hindoo mythology to help him in so small a matter, which some of themselves had, in all probability, placed before him on purpose to see how his nerve or his genius would get over it; and that it was quite vanity to think that they would leave their comfortable quarters in wood, or stone, or brass, to extricate a mortal from difficulties of his own making; that his wit was given him for the purpose of planning, and his sinews to enable him to execute the plot so as to make all straight.

Now this advice was very well taken by Ramdeen, and he repeated it, with additions of his own, to many others, who all thought Hoossein very clever and very good natured to say so much.

Then he went and told Ailee all about it,

and she asked a great deal more about Hoossein, and Ramdeen gave her much valuable information, for which she had a ready market, and some of which cropped up afterwards.

CHAPTER XIII.

CLOUDS.

When two electric clouds meet in the atmosphere, the result is a thunder storm.

Certain combinations within the bosom of this globe, produce earthquakes.

Two currents of water meeting, produce a bore.

As with the elements, so is it with man: there is not room enough for some of them to live together. If they clash in civilized society, the law is called in to smooth down the bore;

if in uncivilized society, then the earth swallows up her prey, with strong convulsions; if in mixed society, the clouds may for a time be heavy, but are eventually scattered by civilization and knowledge.

Meteorologists may foretell storms, but get no credence. When the Sikhs lost their country, in consequence of the pride, the ignorance, and the rapacity of their own soldiery, a similar cloud had for some time been gathering in our own provinces. The storm was foretold, but the prophets of evil were not believed.

When little clouds burst at Rawul Pindee, Jeelum, and Wuzeerebad, the poor Sepoys were told that they were very naughty, and must do their duty better in future; when a Sepoy regiment refused to cross the Sutlej, it was coaxed into compliance by extra leave of absence—the men laughed at the manœuvre; when the Fortress of Gowendghur was seized by a rebellious regiment, it was disbanded, and the men were scattered over the country, as fragments of a thunder cloud are scattered over the sky.

Hoossein found his elements getting so discordant, and his clouds collecting so rapidly, that he became anxious on the subject; his divan was frequented by men eager for the fray, strong, active, drilled men—idle, poor, and proud. He found it difficult to restrain them; they told him that there was no reason for delay, there was nothing to fear; if any Sahebs were left from the slaughter, they would only say, don't do it again! Hoossein argued, that their plans were not matured, that the south and west of India were not drawn within the vortex, that nothing could be done properly, unless all India should join in the common cause.

Some laughed at, and some applauded Hoossein, but while they were talking, and plotting, other currents, combinations, and clouds, were all driving in the right direction.

Hoossein hurried on his preparations. He

saw the signs of the times, and remembered Sambo's advice: "Never throw away an opportunity!"

There was a legend in the army, much talked of at this time, that it might have taken India to itself many years before, when the current of liberality from Lord Combermere, met the current of economy from the Court of Directors, with Lord William Bentinck to guide it, a mighty bore arose, the danger was seen, safety valves were opened, the current of economy flowed over the officers, that of liberality over the Sepoy, who was at once convinced that the Sirkar could not do without him. The vanity of the army retained this legend better than the dusty archives of Leadenhall-street.

Now again, the liberal current was guided by Sir Charles Napier; while that of economy was guided by the inflexible Lord Dalhousie; resolute and self confiding, he refused credence to danger, or if he did believe it, his imperious temper might have wished to bring it to a head, that he in his firmness might subdue it.

Sir Charles Napier, like Lord Combermere, retired from a post, the responsibility of which, was shared in by another. He left his warning of danger behind him, apparently unheeded and unthought of.

So little did Lord Dalhousie think of the rising storm, that he undertook to pay off a heavy sum of the Government debt, from money not fairly available for the purpose, and in a short time he was again compelled to borrow to replace the money he had expended. This finance transaction depreciated the Government securities to such an extent, that much discontent was caused.

Hoossein seized the moment to send emissaries in every direction; his instructions to them were short.

" It is time to rule ourselves ; the date of the old prophecy has expired. The company Sirkar must go ; faith can no longer be reposed in them. All the money was taken out of the country, and they were deceived. The rulers lost their dignity, and disputed with each other. No rewards were given to any one; the territory was increased, but the expenditure was decreased. The Sirkar had got all they wanted, and spurned the men who got it for them. Suttees and adoption were forbidden. Lands were taken from the people; officers and civilians were occupied in conversion. Religions and castes were despised."

Such was the substance of the text; the messengers were instructed to entice all good Mussulmen and all true Hindoos to flock to the rescue of their country.

A wrinkled, hard looking man, a Brúmacharee, undertook to convey the message to the West; there could not have been a better selection; his vow of celibacy procured his admission every where, while his temper and his knowledge peculiarly fitted him for the occasion.

His burden was a heavy one, but while

travelling through the north-west territory and the Nerbuddah districts, he was relieved of it pleasantly enough. The Sepoys, already inoculated, were only wishing the auspicious moment to arrive. The Zemindars were ready, provided their estates were confirmed to them; in fact the Brumacharee was well pleased, for he obtained attentive listeners, and many promised to do as all the rest did.

As he travelled further he found fewer listeners, and no promises.

In the fine old Mohammedan city of Bhorampoor, where the magnificent palaces still shew the splendour of that proud dynasty, he found people who remembered Hoossein; they were not under the Raj of the Company, and thought the subject a very interesting one, and a matter in which they should be very happy to help ; but that such a grand project should be mentioned to them as coming from their rather despised townsman, was, to say the least of it, rather suspicious, considering that he had been drowned many years ago in Calcutta. This remark rather abashed the Brumacharee, who had not been entrusted with the adventure.

There were Purdasee Sepoys at Malligam, the next camp our messenger stopped at, who were glad to hear of their friends in Bengal. He had many remembrances to many people and as long as he told them pleasant anecdotes, such as the wrestling match, and other little affairs arising from it, he had no reason to complain of his reception; but when he came to the pith of the story, the Brumacharee found no sympathy. All were contented with their lot, all had faith in their Sirkar. Their officers were good, so were the paymasters.

"Shew us," they said, "who are better. We have not forgotten the want of faith, and the deficient pay of the Mahratta. We are well off now, and hope to remain so; as long as we do our duty there is no fear of our losing our salt, our pensions, or our caste. It was only yesterday that our Soobedhar was presented with a pair of beautiful silver mounted pistols in public Durbar, as a small acknowldgement of the attention he had given to his duties for many years. If your men in Bengal do not get presents, it confirms the tales we hear, that they do not deserve them. Your message does not concern us, Brumacharee Saheb."

In the villages of Khandesh he met with no success.

"I am an old man now," said one of his audience, " but my memory runs back to village walls, lofty and thick; our population was reckoned by thousands; the people were prosperous, and the cattle covered the hills ; the song of the grinding was heard in the morning, the song of the moat all night, and the sound of the sugar mills in the day ; our looms rattled, our bread was sweet, and our nights were passed in peace. Then came that war which you wish to come again; after the war came the Pindarees, and then the Bheels of the hills ; between these misfortunes all was changed ; the looms and the cotton were burned, the sugar was trodden under foot, the sound of the grinding had ceased, the women were carried off, the men were killed, the children starved, our village walls were broken down, and all our cattle driven away. Now we require no walls, for we have had peace for many years. Outram Saheb Bahadoor gave it to us; he told us that we could keep it as long as we pleased. We live under a good rule; we wish for no change."

The Brumacharee passed on to Nassick, that stronghold of Brahminical intolerance. Here he touched on conversion.

"Look to history," he said, "and see how all conquerors have converted the conquered. The Company Sirkar has beaten all its enemies, taken all their Mooluks; there is nothing else to be done now but to convert us to their own religion, and such a religion that no two men can agree upon it. They will mix us all up together. There are to be no castes: Mussulman, and Hindoo, and Feringhee are to be all the same; they are making iron roads on which to grind those who refuse; and you, men of Nassick, you listen to the Missionary Sahibs, who come to convert you, and make you enemies of your own people. You were good Brahmins once. Your temples and your suttees witness in your favour, yet you will accept conversion, and become apostates to your faith. You will contaminate the waters of your sacred river."

As he spoke the last word he stopped, disturbed by a commotion in the audience making way for an old man who was getting down from the pedestal of a pillar, and crying out in feeble tones for the Brumacharee to stop.

"Hold!" cried the old man, trembling with agitation, "we are not apostates, though we can do without our Suttees. The incremation never was an ordinance of our Shaster; but it had grown into a horrid custom, originating with those who objected to maintain the widow. I, for one, am glad that the act of Suttee is forbidden. We stand in no danger of conversion from the Missionary Sahebs who come amongst us; they have been pleasant people, with whom I loved to hold converse; their house is like a mine of polished diamonds, their conversation like a string of pearls, their anecdotes are like the trickling streams, and their breath like the whispers of the breezes in the spring; as to their religion, I tell them they are vain to think that they only know the truth; they tell me that I am bigoted; I tell them that mine is the oldest religion, that theirs is a new one, incomprehensible even to themselves ; there is no fear of our Nassick Missionaries converting any one who has an idea of his own, or bread to eat. Now, as for contaminating our sacred river, which flows from the Ghey Mookh (cow's mouth), we shall not do it; but were it not for that misfortune, I would advise you, Mr. Brumacharee, to do as our young men are now doing, look at them going down the foaming wave, and passing through the narrow pass on the smooth falling water into the troubled basin down below; it might cleanse you from your sins. I am sorry to cast discredit on any one, especially on a sacred character, and I am ready to believe that the facts are as you have stated them, on your side of India; here they are different, neither officers nor civilians exert themselves to make converts; they are strictly prohibited from doing so; moreover, if any cases come before magistrate or judge, in which a question of religion arises, it is referred to the Shastrie or the Moolah for their opinion. If religious questions are not so managed with you, I think you have a grave cause of complaint."

The Brumacharee had been getting very uneasy, when the washing was alluded to; but, after a few common-place expressions, as to his pleasure at finding them all so happy and contented, he bade the circle adieu, and went on his way.

In a few days he arrived at Poona, where he found old friends of his own, and friends of the Peshwa's family, remembrances of whom he had brought with him from Benares. There were the Bhosla, the Rastia, the Vinchoorken, the Putwurdur houses, and many others, who held high state in years gone by, supplying large quotas of troops to the army of the Peshwa—their influence was all gone; they had no authority; all were in decay, and the messenger felt that it would not do to open all his plans to those who had lost their energy and ability, and deemed themselves contented to live under a foreign sway, with scarcely a remembrance of their lost power. In consideration of all this, he attempted to feel his way with the question of adoption.

"That is a melancholy subject to many of us," said a sunken-eyed, hollow-cheeked, old man; "that is how the company's Raj obtains provinces. They have only lately obtained the principality of Peint, in that way; and there are many others that I could mention. It is hard on the people to prevent a continuance of the name, if fate has denied a son."

The Brumacharee thought he was rather successful at Poona, and went rejoicing on his beautiful journey to Sattera. He looked at the magnificent reservoir, which formerly supplied Poona with water; but now the Katrass Lake was nearly silted up. The old paved road, over the mountain, was broken down, and nearly gone; but the magnificent temple of Whie remained, with its shady tree, and its clear river, and its cholera climate. He met friends here, who gladly escorted him on to the city.

Here everything exceeded his most sanguine hopes. The old native gentlemen hated the existing state of things; they had not forgotten the Rajah, and all the amusements of that Mahratta court; they had forgotten the military power of the British, and thought how easy it would be to destroy them. Vain people, when the time came, they were held in check by one civilian.

From Sattara the Brumacharee went on to Beljaumun and Darwa. Here, for the first time, he was glad to find that Mahratta sepoys were ready to listen to the voice of reason. There had been disturbances in these districts not many years previous, and a spirit of discontent was still abroad. Recruits had been raised from these people, who were now in the regiments stationed there. They were still sore with the unexpected defeat they had met with in their mountain fortress; and in spite of their fresh oath of servitude, they were ready to follow anyone to independence or plunder. They were urgent for immediate action, and there was some difficulty in obtaining their promise to await the signal.

Here also the Brumacharee found allies amongst the cultivators—men whose enams had been resumed; whose friends and adherents, after living on them all their lives, were now driven to work for their daily bread—all of these were ready to aid in the good cause, provided their estates were guaranteed to them.

"You had better not!" interposed a wise-looking, consequential Mussulman. "I was once in the service of the Sirkar. I was dismissed for peculation. I tried every possible way of getting back again. I was told that bribery could do everything. I spent all my money; and here I am a wiser and, I hope, a better man, with a tolerable knowledge of the power that rules us—of its honesty and its determination. Did you ever consider that you ill-treated the Sirkar every moment in which you held your enams beyond the term of tenure? Do you not see how leniently you have been treated, in not having to pay up arrears? Only think what a native government would have done. What ransom would you have given for your noses, if you had held the enam one day longer than your sunnud allowed you? You had service tenures, improving tenures, and time tenures. Some of these were given, when the Government which gave them was tottering to the fall, when those who signed the papers never knew what they were doing; yet all these doubtfully obtained possessions have been confirmed to you as they were found; and many of you have enjoyed them far beyond the time allowed. None of you have improved them, and none of you have done the services for which they were given. It is, I allow, a strong cause of enmity, to be forcibly deprived of what you unjustly kept; but with all your ill-will to the rulers, you can scarcely wish to bring back on yourselves troubles worse than those you endured a few years ago. You have not forgotten how grateful you were to Outram Saheb Bahadoor, for reducing Mansintosh so quickly. The only difference in your feelings is this,—that whereas at that time you thought you had something to lose, now you know that you have nothing; yet would it be well to remember that your neighbours have."

A murmur of approbation followed this speech, and the Brumacharee thought to himself, " this Outram Saheb must be a great man; I hear of him everywhere." So he went on to Bellary.

The old man's pony had but little rest here. The Madras Sepoys were happy and contented—their cantonments were small colonies—wives, sweethearts, and children, he had never seen anything like it in Bengal. He travelled on to Bangalore; it was the same thing over again—content was everywhere.

After a long, hot, and feverish journey, he, at last, reached Vellore. Here he was talking of the necessity of a change—of the evils poured down on their poor heads—of the pleasures everyone enjoyed under a Government of their own construction. He was in the midst of his warmest harangue, when he was interrupted by a loud stamping on the floor.

A grey-haired, white-bearded pensioner, with a wooden leg, was stumping up towards him. He was partially paralyzed, and nearly blind.

"I have come close to you," he said, as he touched the Brumacharee, " that my poor old eyes may see the man who ventures to talk as you do. I am old—very old. I have been a pensioner for thirty years. My leg was shot off at Pegu. I have seen many wars, and I have known brave men. I am not a coward myself; but I have never known so brave a man as you. When I was young, the Sepoys talked as you do now. They were many, and they encouraged one another; but you stand here alone, and incite your hearers to deeds of valour—against whom? Do you know that, on the very ground where you now stand, I have seen vast heaps of mutineers—dead, festering in the sunshine? I have forgotten many things since that day, but it returns now on my memory, as the blossoms that come in the spring time. Gillespie Saheb was the man to do and to dare. The silly men were mowed from the face of the earth, as the corn is mowed by the mower. One event of that

M

kind lasts for a long life, and I never wish such a thing to happen again. You had better take your departure. I have seen you, and I understand you—go!"

The Brumacharee did go; he had collected all he could. The rivulets of discontent were few in the circle entrusted to him; but he hastened back to Bengal, to add his cloud to the heavy atmosphere, and to aid his friends to the utmost of his power, in bringing on the approaching earthquake.

CHAPTER XIV.

THE SIGNAL.

CURRENTS were running in all directions, thunder clouds gathered around, and a rumbling sound in the atmosphere proclaimed the approach of a storm.

From the borders of fair Cashmere, from the Himalaya mountains, from beyond the Indus, and from far Kurachee, his messengers had some time since returned to Hoossein. There had been many meetings, and much talk.

Hoossein was well pleased with most of what he heard. If now and then a doubt disturbed him, he threw it fiercely aside; if the intemperate zeal of the Sepoys harassed him, he said "their blood be upon their own heads; they shall not disturb my great work." He had only one object in life, and he was doing it. His heart was alive with hope, and so eager with expectation, that he saw not the obstacles in his way; he was a fine example of human nature, as sketched by his great progenitor the prophet: "man is weak."

Hoossein lay stretched on his red and green sutringe, with his face, as he hoped, towards Mecca; he was going through the ordinary prayers of a devout Mahomedan; no one knew how to lay his carpet with greater propriety; no one could prostrate himself with greater ease or grace; he had studied the attitude—the clasping of his hands, the upturning of his eyes, and the movement of his lips, were all done with thought and with a purpose.

No one would doubt the truth of a man, who was such an attentive observer of outward forms. There were many who watched him, many who copied him; but while Hoossein was thanking God and His Prophets for throwing his enemies into his clutches, and for enabling him to be the humble means of liberating his country, they thought that he was only doing as he said he was, praying for forgiveness of his past offences.

"*What thou doest do,*" was Hoossein's motto. He did not care how.

There was another man in the east, who held a smilar motto, "*ora et Labora.*" In high position, with simple faith and honesty he laboured. His prayers had been heard, his enemies had disappeared, his empire had increased, the ten talents entrusted to his care had multiplied. There was no danger now; his kingdom was complete; his vision was filled with far-off scenes of recompense and reward, which might well engross his faculties; he had been in the east long enough to understand the intrigues of Asiatics. There was no danger while he was there; he was equal to any occasion, and took but little notice of the forebodings of evil around him; he, in person, could never come in contact with such as Hoossein. But he could not remain for ever. His time of service was nearly over.

It will be for the historian to tell us, how far his desire to serve two masters—the East India Company and the people of England—drove Lord Dalhousie into the narrow groove; suffice it for me to say, that with acquisition on one side, and economy on the other, with the danger of these elements fairly laid before him, he refused to take precautions. He would not see things as they were; he had reached India when affairs in general were on the change. He laboured hard to perfect those changes. The overland communication with England had been brought nearly to perfection, railroads were winding their level paths through the valleys, over the mountains; electric wires whispered unheard from one end of the territory to the other; strange things were growing rapidly before the eye of the Asiatic; but mythical legends were departing, and plain matter of fact supervening; the delicacy of touch the fine handling, were all gone; the filmy veil was ruthlessly drawn aside by decided hands; a picture was disclosed to the oriental, harsh, and unpleasing ; but like a pre-Raphaelite, it had much truth in it.

" 'Coming events cast their shadows before them!'" exclaimed Hoossein. "Let all be destroyed; let us cast them all together in the sea," hissed out his low voice, as snake-like he entered the divan, where the Brumacharee had promised to meet him.

They had met in private since the messengers' return; and in a long midnight talk, with only one small lamp shining in dim splendour upon them, these two men, a cunning Brahmin, and a determined Mahomedan, reconstructed and manufactured a fable, which, in their vanity, was to ruin one dynasty, and set up another. The outlines had been picked up in his travels, and the hard old bachelor thought he could fill up his sketches to the satisfaction of any eastern audience.

As the Brumacharee entered the long saloon, with its low, dark ceiling, supported on carved wooden pillars, the evening light pouring softly in through the narrow windows, on a red and blue carpet, spread from end to end of the room. He was aware of a very villanous-looking company; audacious men were there, some in their own beautiful costume, some in the uniform of their masters, whom they still served, and whose salt they still eat and whose eyes they blinded with dust of obedience; there were rich muslin turbans, and gay shawls from Cashmere; satin piejamis, and gold about the slippers; the wearers representing landholders, idlers, and representatives of each arm of the kala pultun of Bengal—men in a good service, with ample pay for their small wants, with little to do, and a pension in a not distant horizon—all of them hanging the skirts of their hope on the heartrending thorns of discontent and treason; and the girdles of their faith on the avalanche of that oriental charity which had been falling and crushing their forefathers, long before history could remember.

Hoossein was standing at the further end; he was a fine-looking fellow, in the prime of life; his hair was slightly tinged with grey, but his beard and moustache were black as jet, and beautifully polished.

He took the Brumacharee by the hand, and standing by one of the pillars, he said, in a clear voice,

"Here, my friends, is the man who has just returned from his feathered journey to the west and to the south; his little plumes have grown into the feathers of an eagle, and each has had the eyes of the peacock; his feet have rivalled the fleetness of the antelope, and his tales, like the wondrous legends of Arabia, will set your hearts at rest. Hear what he has to say, my friends, and then judge to how many millions of our race your success will be like the sunshine succeeding a thunderstorm."

The Brumacharee, standing by Hoossein's side, began,

"My tale is like the summer drought; the moisture of the country is gone, the herbage is withered, the sticks are gathered, they will not kindle in the flame, and no smoke arises.

"The poor Mahratta has but three garments, his coarse pugree, his home spun cumlie, and his unbleached langootee, everything else, his lota, and his cooking utensils are with the Soucar. He is his slave; from him he gets his daily bread; from him comes the marriage festival for the son, the beggar. The hearts of the people are sick, and a great medicine is needed.

" Princes, with time honoured names, have

risen in the hills to put down this oppression of the Soucars; their noses have been taken from them, and some have been burnt in the fires of Jehannum, so that their names have been lost on their accounts; the poor people would have become free, but then came the evil Genü, who hover o'er this land; the Princes were destroyed, the oppressors were encouraged.

"Listen to the tale of the Western Ghauts!

"Rajogee Bangria is pursued; his life is required to sacrifice at the shrine of oppression; he is a fugitive in the jungle.

"A follower of his is caught and is ordered to betray his master.

"He replied: 'I will! when the darkness of night has made them secure; when their feet are weary with the march; when sleep is upon them, I will shew the Saheb the resting place of my master; when I say "Now!" then will the Saheb, and his army rush on, and secure all he finds.

"The paths are narrow, the mountains

high, the precipices steep, and the night is dark and stormy.

"The fearless follower, with a pistol held to his head, guides the Saheb in safety; 'they are close,' he whispers; then, with a voice which echoes from rock to rock, from wood to wood, he cries out, 'Now!' and dashes on.

Amidst the distant echoes of his frantic cry, other sounds come up from the deep abyss—sounds like the sighs of those who go to Jehannum. A curse was howled out from the faithful man, as he fell alone, and found that no one had followed to the resting place.

"The shapeless mass of the true man, who would not betray his master, is still unburied amidst those mountain dells. He must be avenged—the mountain coolie expects his sun to rise.

"Listen to the tyranny to the Sirkar. The people of S——t groaned beneath the sceptre of a cruel native; their backs were broken; there were heavy burdens on their heads in the hot sunshine; pepper bags were tied on their faces; hot pincers tore their tender bodies; their toe nails were pulled out; their houses were burned, and their goods plundered; their hearts sang the silent songs of sorrow, and the Tyrant was dressed in robes of white.

"It happened that a good Saheb (an exception to the rule), one of those who worked for the people, and not for himself, whose beacon was built on the rock of honesty, proposed to draw out the teeth of the oppressor.

"'I have no teeth! My lips are of honey; my hands are bathed in the purity of the morning dew; let the curse of dismissal fall on the head of my calumniator,' cried the Tyrant.

"The teeth of derision rattled in the mouth of the liar; the good Saheb was put on the shelf of poverty, and the streets of the city were washed with the tears of bitterness.

"A white Tyrant sat on the seat of judgment.

A debtor was brought before him; he could not pay—he was ill; he could not explain— he was beaten; his very weakness was used against him, so he departed to the world where there are no debts.

"The wings of the white man were clipped, but they grew again. Justice flew away on the wings of night; the Tyrant was liberated; he smiled neath the eye of his ruler. Let the fish-hooks of remorse enter his heart, and the ghost of the dead man hold the lines.

"White gloves and garments are worn by the dealers in Khutput; they wear their shoes in the palaces, and smile on the ladies within them. Sore is the foot of him who tried, in his justice, to curb them. Outram the great is gone, sunk in his contest with Khutput; songs are now dipped in blood—songs of this Sirdar, this Rustum, this Outram is nobody now. Khutput will help you to slay him."

"We can do that without help," cried more than one voice from the listening circle.

The Brumacharee smiled a strange smile, and continued,

"The dignity of nobles has departed; they fight with themselves, instead of working for the people; bribery and corruption defile the names of the rulers.

"There are no longer good governors; the light of truth and respectability has departed.

"Our money flows away like the waters of the Ganges, and never comes back again. They are perpetually coining fresh rupees, and each coinage has more alloy.

"The Sirkar is rapacious, and takes from the people the gifts that were given for good conduct; the name of the Sirkar is odious, and the land is covered with groaning.

"There are fine cities, palaces, mosques, and temples; there are hill caves and mountain forts, the gateways of which have been destroyed by the white man; their consciences told them they might be used against them: you can take all these forts as easy as you scale your beds.

"There is much wealth scattered over the land; the women and children are covered with gold, silver, and jewels; the English wish to get it all: the sooner it falls into other hands the better.

"The Parsees are friends of the English; they have great houses, much wealth, and broad lands, but they spend thoughtlessly! their property should be taken care of.

"There are pleasant herbs growing on the hills of Sattara: it is a rich country, and requires cultivation.

"What can we expect of a Sirkar with new names—names unknown to our fathers, who wore silk and satins, when theirs were painted, and wore skins for dresses, who now call us niggers? They come thousands of miles to rule us, because the road is easy, and they want our money; yet these men cannot rule us, because they are subservient to others in England, of whom we know nothing except by report; the examples before us give us a bad idea of the whole.

"These men call themselves free—that is, every one does as he likes; a liberty which has ere now brought confusion in its train; their sovereign has no proper control over them; they are always divided into two parties, neither of which ever succeeds in doing right; their rulers are selected by the length of their purses; they call themselves the representatives of the people, and they talk a great deal about India, and control our affairs; they take from, or add to the authority of our government, and they sometimes talk of taking it all away; between the two parties we can get nothing done; our Governor-General Saheb is no longer a man of power, what he does is undone; there is no authority over us; if we do as we please, we are sure to please one of the home parties; so, as we have no proper ruler, let Hoossein Saheb Bahadoor, or the King of Delhi, be our King; both of them are wise and generous—let us serve them."

The Brumacharee was interrupted by

sounds of approbation, and a confused talking.

When silence was obtained, the old man resumed.

"Let us, I say, select our own rulers—rulers to whom we can tell our own wants; who will be on the spot to attend to them; who will rule us as we love to be ruled, as Asiatics must be ruled, honestly and decidedly.

"I have made a long journey; I have braved the hot winds, and the south-west monsoon; I would sooner, my friends, live under the everlasting inconvenience of either of these natural inflictions than under the rule of those whom nature never imposed upon us; down with them now that you have the power! submit no longer to those whose very weakness invites you to their destruction, whose very blindness bids you lead them into the pit! down with them! let them be as the dust of the burning desert, or as the spray of the stormy sea."

The Brumacharee stopped for a moment, then, making a low salam to the company, he continued,

"Is a stronger breeze required to fan the flame? You will soon have it. Let the whirlwind sweep up the spray and the dust; let neither be seen again upon earth; let us eat our own bread, and let us rule ourselves; let the time come when the ever-springing Lotus is bright on the face of the waters. I have said it!"

There was a murmur of assent; the assembly gave themselves to gravity, and the sound of the hubble-bubble increased.

At this moment a well-dressed Chuprassie stepped up to Hoossein with a note.

"See!" cried Hoossein, with a smile, "how our destiny works out our wishes. See how that little wire sends its message through all space in a moment of time. There is, my friends, a war in Persia; all the white army left Bombay this morning, in ships, for the Persian Gulph; all the rest of the white army of India has to go there. Some of the Bombay Kala Pultun has also gone. No Sepoys of the Bengal army will ever go over the Kala Panee again."

He was stopped by loud applause.

"The Persians," continued Hoossein, "are Mahomedans! Some of you, my brothers, fought against the Afghans; they were of your own faith. You were excused on account of your ignorance; this cannot be your plea again. None of you will go to this war, but when the pure Lotus rises from the bosom of the purer stream, be ready! And now I earnestly request your attention to the few more words I have to say to you."

CHAPTER XV.

THE SERPENT.

Hoossein paused for a few moments, during which the assembly moved, settling themselves into attitudes of deep attention.

The silver stick in waiting having then called out,

" Listen, O ye nobles, to the words of the world creator, the eternal justice, the saviour of the universe, the father of wisdom, the holy Seyud Hoossein Ben Hassan Saheb

Bahadoor. God is great, and Mahomed is his prophet; blessed be God!"

For another moment Hoossein stood counting his beads, and scanning the congregation with a careful eye; then, with a humble mien and a quiet voice, he began.

"I wish," he said, "this grand occasion had fallen to the lot of some one who would have been more capable than myself of doing justice to it.

"The poor attention which I have been able to bestow upon the subject has been interrupted by many things, over which I had no co ntrol. I have travelled far and fast, I have communed with your brethren in all places; I have sent emissaries into distant lands; they have collected intelligence, and spread in secret your wishes. I have spared neither time nor trouble in obtaining a knowledge of those things so necessary for our undertaking. I know where the guns and the small arms are kept; I have discovered the magazines and the commissariat stores.

I know the number of guards on all, and I understand how they may be secured; I know the customs of the English, and I see how easily they may be destroyed. When I have detailed to you the reasons for their destruction, you will be able to comprehend how necessary it is, for our own safety as well as for the safety of those who come after us, that it should be done speedily, and with secresy.

"You have all heard of the iniquitous proceedings, the corrupt practices, the undignified conduct of some of our rulers; you have heard how our religious rites are interfered with, and our old customs are abolished; how meanness and rapacity go hand in hand, and liberality and generosity are forgotten.

"I have more to tell you, to enable you to see the full light of our misfortunes, to make you comprehend the full greatness of ourselves, the insignificance of those who oppress us, and the necessity of getting rid of this miserable oppression.

"Many years ago, when peace reigned over the land, when the drum, and the fife, and the bugle were silent, it was attempted to reduce the pay of the army; but your brethren of those days resented it, and flew to arms; then their pay was continued; but that of the white man was reduced. You were of more value than the officer—there was something left for you to do.

"Since that time whole regions have been gained to the Sirkar by your exertions, yet no reward, no enams, no dresses, have been bestowed on you—not even a medal. Your pay is likely to decrease, while the price of food is on the increase. If there was anything more for you to do, you would be safe; but nothing is left to be done here.

"See how this plundering propensity progresses; see how Hindoos, Sikhs, Rajpoots, and Mahomedans are all brought under the sway of this insatiable foreigner.

"A few years ago there was a Saheb—Secunder Burnes—sent on a spying mission to endeavour to deceive them whom it was death to play with. This man was well received everywhere (for the name of the English was great at a distance); he eat the salt of friendship, while the mantle of safety was held above his head.

" This false man was the advance guard of deceitful actions. Province after province, that he visited, was attacked by the English; even the distant region of Afghanistan was invaded, and while the Kaffir caressed the daughters of the north, behold the avenger was upon them; their limbs shivered in the cold, their faces were as white as the snow—there was no place of safety, no sun to warm them.

" Secunder Burnes Saheb was sent to those regions that reward deception.

" The child, Macnaghten Saheb, who had been entrusted with the conduct of the business, was found asleep by a single Mahomedan, who at mid day, in the midst of his army, slaughtered him with impunity.

"The white haired general of the army mingled his worn out locks with the snows of Khyber Pass his brains were gone before; but his head believed an Afghan—an enemy!

"My friends, let us leave children and old men to take care of our women at home.

"The sword of the Mahomedan has been red on the tip with the blood of the white men; let it now be red to the hilt.

"Some one may ask why the Sirkar attacked such distant countries. It is difficult to say. It has been said that the Russ King was at ennaity with it, and was seeking the friendship of the Mahomedan of the mountains; but I look on it as like the fable of the wolf and the lamb at the water; the wolf wanted all, and so did the Sirkar. Who, I ask, was this Russ, this Rustom? Who, with the aid even of the mountaineers, could have injured India, if you, my friends, having been treated properly, fought for the Sirkar? It was a false fable, and under its deceitful feathers the Mahomedan was led against his brother, and your comrades were swallowed up in the snow drifts of the bitter north; there was a grievous wrong done to both of us. True, it was avenged; but it is our duty to see that we are not so used again; it is not right that the Asiatic should pander to the deceit of the European.

"Look around: it is all fraud, violence, and rapacity. Scinde, far away beyond the Indus, our natural boundary, has been seized, on the plea that it was badly governed. What does this mean? Only that it did not belong to them; the Government was of no importance to the English, but they wished to get the revenues of a province, which were then expended in itself. No one ever complained of a bad government, and if they had done so, what right had the white man to take away the little sunshine which was left?

"Look at the Punjaub. We all knew the old lion who held it so long and so well. While he lived our Sirkar was his friend: his teeth were sharp, his claws were strong;

when he died there was talk of annexation. The Kalsa Fouj was strong, but the whelps had not the wisdom of the old lion; so, although they poured down upon our territory like the avalanche of the mountain, yet you drove them back again like the chaff before the wind. You defended the land of the stranger from fire and sword; you slaughtered the enemy in great battles; the plains were covered with his corpses, and the rivers ran red with their blood.

"You will now reap the reward of your sacrifices and of your valour. You will be reduced. There are no enemies left. You will not go across the Kala Panee, and as they seek for foes there now, they will get other men for their soldiers. The news is come that a great army is gone, or going to Persia; let us not lose our opportunity.

"There was once on a time a Mahomedan Ameer, with the wisdom of Seuliman and the forethought of the prophet, blessed be his name! He also received the spy, Secunder

Bures, with kindness and hospitality, and listened to his honey words of deceit. He looked, and behold! his neighbours were gone; the kings of the countries visited by Burnes were fugitives, like antelopes scattered by the wolf; they had no place to rest on, their ground was taken from their feet.

"When his eyes were dry from their weeping, he looked again, and behold! one of the Feringhees was in his toils—Colonel Stoddart Saheb—what did he do there? alone, far from his own people. Did the English do things without an object? Never! They shall get nothing from me!

"So he looked out with a smile, for Stoddart Saheb was safe; and lo! another spy wandered through the land, the sunshine of pleasure on his face, the moonlight of folly on his brow.

"As the decoy bird entices the wild one, so the false pen of Stoddart lured Connolly into the nets of the Ameer, who stretched out the sharp sabre of caution, and struck off the heads of the false ones.

"This Ameer is safe in his kingdom; the English prefer fighting against Persians, who have done them no harm, while Bokhara has killed their people.

"Let us, I repeat, never lose an opportunity, and never neglect so bright an example; let your blades be sharp, and your aims be true; your country has been long in the hands of the alien, but our hearts are free; let them no longer be hung up in the bonds of slavery. The African was a slave, but is now free; his own right hand procured his freedom, and the fickle councils of England confirmed it. Why should not we be free, and living like the Africans, in ease, indolence, and plenty?

"Think of the miserable pittance you get; think on what you may obtain; make up your mind to get it; be wise as serpents, but secret as the cat.

"I tell you that the signal for the rising is

gone forth—the bread to tell you that every man must get his own; the lotus to tell you when to rise: when that fair divinity, the symbol of creation, appears on the waters, then is our time; then communication will be difficult, and travelling impossible.

" Time flies rapidly, but be patient; curb your own, curb the impatience of those you meet. If we are rash, and act hastily, all will be lost, and a hundred years will have passed in vain.

" Be patient, and be united; be firm and be collected, and I, Hoossein Ben Hassan, will promise you a freedom you have never dreamed of. No longer shall your caste rites be infringed on; no longer shall the shadow of the infidel fall upon your bread; no longer shall the circumcised be the slave of the un-circumcised. Our women shall be our own; we will do as we please with our wives and children. In short, my friends, we will no longer eat the bitter cake of bondage, for the white man shall be gone, and we shall be at liberty."

Hoossein ceased speaking.

The assembly had been held as a secret one; all outward signs of approbation had been strictly forbidden, yet was there again a murmur loud and continued, words of praise and signs of encouragement; there were men who stood up to say a word, but it was all repetition, except one sentence, and that was spoken by a man whom no one knew; it was short and suggestive.

"If," said the voice, "we are successful, I will give Hoossein Saheb Bahadoor a golden serpent; if we are not, he will find a live one."

CHAPTER XVI.

THE DAUGHTERS OF DELHI.

KHOODA BUX brought in his master's breakfast; there was much familiarity between them, and the servant said,

"Did Hoossein Saheb see the carriage pass? —a carriage with two gazelles inside, whose pearly teeth were not hidden by the rose leaves around them—whose eye lashes glitter in perpetual sunshine."

"I saw no carriage," replied Hoossein; "my thoughts are busy with serious matters."

"While the master is eating his breakfast, may his slave wander to the gates of Paradise, and discover who those fair houris may be? he may bring back something to awake his lord from his sadness."

Khooda Bux walked out with a curious expression on his ugly face.

"There must be something going on, or I should not have been allowed to go."

Hoossein dipped his fingers in his rice and eat. His pillau was good; he eat slowly, and then stopping, as if weary with the exertion, he rested his chin on his hand.

"It is my fate," he muttered to himself, "every thing within and without tends to one point; streamlets starting from the same place will take opposite courses. The Indus and the Ganges have their sources in the same hills, but their waters sweeten very distant seas. The European and the Indian have different origins, yet are they running in one direction, and will enter the unknown Kala Pani together. It is a salt sea, its waves are bitter, heaving, and undefined; there are rocks beneath its bosom, rough and hard, breaking to pieces those who are dashed against them. The tempest is commencing, foam is already seen on the breaking wave, the wild bird screams with joy, and flits about on the swift pinions of expectation; the wild fox and the jackal sit howling on the sand covered shores of hope."

Hoossein eat a little, and drank some cool water, then relapsed into his train of thought.

"Strange! I devised this ruin, but I asked not that they should aid in their own destruction. How is it that they help me? As it was with the negro, so is it with us. There are people in England who advocate our cause, who wish us to be put in high places, and to rule our own people —who wish to destroy the Sirkar as it now exists. How is this? Where did the idea come from? Did some demon of discontent whisper it in the ears of the credulous. Let there be a change, they say, let the wings of the old company be clipped ; divide the power (aye, and the spoil); let us know what is going on, and keep some control over them. Good! What control can distant England keep over us? While the Punchayet talks it forgets that we are not consulted. Our affairs are mentioned, and we are supposed capable of great things, such as ruling ourselves; but none of us are admitted into that Punchayet, which claims to itself the power of controlling us. It is high time for us to make a Punchayet of our own.

"Sambo was a true oracle ; there are two parties: one wishes to rule us, the other that we should rule ourselves. The latter speaks with a hidden object, the former do not know how to rule Asiatics. It will never do to send a great man to rule our army, and another great man to rule him, and other greater men to control him, and a king or queen to govern all. The centralisation of power in so distant a place is an error; there should be a supreme ruler in each province.

My Sirdars shall be in plenty, and each shall govern his district with a rod of iron. It is said in England that the Mahomedan is lazy, and incapable of work. Ah! ah! they shall see! They talk of work, when every thing is done by Khutput, and the money owners take their complaints to England. They had better go to Jehannum. They talk of abolishing our language, our weights and measures. The only good the men have done is removing the Lord Saheb, the only man I ever feared, and have sent out a Governor-General Saheb, who will make us all Christians if he can; he will have railroads, fire and water to help him; then those talking wires —ah! it will give him the power of Shitan."

Hoossein started, he had been so intent on his subject, that he had not heard a footstep approaching.

"It is only me," said Khoda Bux, with a smile. "Did you expect him of whom you were talking to come and help you to finish your uneaten breakfast?"

"I was not speaking, was I?" asked Hoossein.

"Well, it was more a hiss than a talk; but one word was very audible," said Khoda Bux. "I have come to tell what I have seen, and perhaps my master will change his mind as to the company he wishes to see. Did you ever, Hoossein Saheb, see the picture of the Beebe Sahibs in the palace of Delhi?"

Hoossein said nothing; he had seen the originals of more than one picture.

Khoda Bux went on,

"She is the Tara of the picture, with the same youth, beauty, and vivacity; he painted the very length of eye lashes, and the graceful shape of her arm. There is a little difference, for the picture has mild eyes, while the real one has the fiery eyes of Hoossein Saheb. I saw them flash as she was told that she could not enter the house, because the Beebe Saheb Ameena was there.

"If my master is thinking of other things, and his inclination turns not towards the new flowers of creation, then Khoda Bux will go."

"Go on," said Hoossein. "Where did she go to?"

"She staid there."

"How was that?"

"Her will! She said she must; she had been told to stay there, so she would stay. I offered my services to her attendants, to get the baggage into the house—such dresses, such jewellery, such shawls of cashmere, scattered about the hackery; and all come from Delhi."

"Did you say her name was Tara?"

"I did; and a Tara she is."

"What did you say about Ameena?"

"I said she was in the house."

"Well, what about her?"

"Not much. While the other Beebe talked to the people, she looked out of the window, and seeing the face below, cried out that, if she could find room, she was welcome to come in. I went upstairs. She sat at breakfast with her daughters, the two moonbeams; and Tara Saheb, finding they were Mahomedans, sat down with them. All her servants had not arrived, as there was some tumasha on the road—execution, or something of that sort. There has been a boberie somewhere."

"How old are the daughters?" asked Hoossein.

"I suppose, from fourteen to sixteen years."

"What is Ameena like?"

"Why do you ask about her, when the other beebe is here. Go and see them, Saheb, and judge for yourself."

"How came they here?"

"Tara Saheb is come from Delhi. I was told she has come from Hoossein Lushkeree."

"Hoossein Luskheree, the wise man. Ah! I will see these beebe Sahebs."

In the evening of that day, Hoossein dressed himself in a new white muslin dress, fitting close to his neck. The sleeves were tight below the elbows, and were rolled, in many wrinkles, round his arm; the green satin vest showed through the thin muslin; a green, gold-embroidered shawl, was folded neatly round his waist; his turban was of fine white Delhi tissue, one end of which, fringed with golden threads, hung over his left shoulder; a pair of silver-mounted pistols were partly concealed in, and an ivory-hilted dagger was conspicuous in front of his kumer bund.

Hoossein had received many visitors that day; they came in a hurry, and went away with seeming anxiety, expressing some doubts as to Hoossein's sincerity in the great cause. Whatever he may have felt, however anxious the intelligence he heard might have made him, nothing could be gained from his face; it was never more composed than when he went up to the house pointed out by the servant.

"Could he see the Tara Saheb," he asked, "on business of great importance?"

He was asked what business.

"A Bijlee message from Hoossein Lushkeree."

Hoossein was then conducted upstairs. There was a dim light from one window, and strong scent of sandal wood oil. Two females sat on a low divan.

Hoossein salaaming low, said, "a friend of Hoossein Lushkeree is come to pay his respects to his daughter, and to tell her that the great man, who lives in the sunshine of the King of the Universe, has, by his wonderful knowledge of the stars, foreseen that the sun and the moon are about to change places. Discord will happen in the transit. He wishes that the Tara who guides the mariner should not be disturbed, and requires her to shine at Plassey immediately—to go towards it this very night."

"How am I to know that this is true?" asked the lady.

Hoossein made a sign, which was recognised.

" When must I go ?"

" Now. Great things are in progress. You must make haste; the hand of man is small to guide so fair a star. Delay not, for your dear life's sake !"

There was an impressive kindness in the last words which attracted the attention of Tara.

" May I not wait till to-morrow ?" she asked.

" If a star stops in its course, it drops from Heaven. See," said Hoossein, pointing into the night, "there is a misguided star, which has fallen from its high abode, and rushes through empty space into utter darkness--its place knows it no more. The daughter of Delhi will go where knowledge guides her."

" Where shall I go!" exclaimed the alarmed girl.

" To Plassey. Everything is arranged; your attendants are prepared; your vehicle is ready ; the friend of the Lushkeree takes his leave of the daughter of Delhi."

So they parted, the attendant whispering,

"That man is the very image of yourself, Tara Saheb."

"I wish I was as beautiful," she said.

Hoossein walked quietly downstairs. At the street-door he met a man, to whom he handed a bag of money, saying, "See, Sooltan, that my daughter of Delhi reaches Plassey in safety. I have written to Mohamed to receive her. When you have done this, join me at Delhi as soon as possible. Time is short; and I find that while I am working to make the centre sound, and our foundation strong, some one is working wheels which may destroy all my contrivances. Even I may not be in time; and she—ah! see, Sooltan, that she reaches in safety. The night is dark; see that she does not stumble."

As he spoke, the females came—a glare of torchlight fell on their veiled faces. Hoossein touched gently the hem of a garment; the vehicle, with the white bullocks, drove on, and Hoossein retired into a lower chamber.

CHAPTER XVII.

THE OLDEST FRIENDS.

"Where is the Beebe Ameena?" said Hoossein, to an attendant, when the bustle of the departure was over.

"Gone to her repose," was the reply.

"Awake her, and tell her that her oldest friend upon earth will be glad to speak to her, on a very important subject."

The servant, startled at the imperious order, did as she was bid.

"Is it Ameena, the daughter of Yusuff Hadji, that I am speaking to?" enquired Hoossein.

"May the daughter of Yusuff ask who it is that speaks to her?" said Ameena.

"A spirit of olden days," was the quiet reply, "come to tell you that your father is dead, and to ask you, what has become of Hoossein, your betrothed?"

"He was drowned!"

"And your husband, Ibrahim?"

"He is dead!"

"And where is Eglington Saheb?"

"He is dead also," said the woman, trembling, but she mastered her weakness, and said in firm voice, "who is the spirit of olden days, who is my oldest friend upon earth? On what subject would he wish to speak? Ameena, the daughter of Yusuff, listens!"

"Does Ameena remember the Caves of Ellora and the Roza of the Dervish?"

"I do."

"Does she remember the wild flowers

growing on the steep rocks, the little short lived flowers of blue?"

" Yes, I remember them."

" And the sweet honey from the rocks. Who got the honey for Ameena, and who made the wreaths of little flowers?"

" Yes, I remember, Hoossein made the wreaths, and he got the honey; it was very sweet."

" Who was it that brought the pretty little quail to Ameena?"

" Hoossein !"

" Who was it that fell into the water at Ellera, while getting the pure white lotus for Ameena?—and did Ameena weep when he was brought insensible to the shore?"

" Oh, yes ! I remember I wept, because I thought my friend Hoossein had gone away."

" Does Ameena recollect a little white fawn, that fed from her hand, and slept on her carpet?—did Ameena weep when it was stolen away?"

" Ameena did weep."

"Ameena had a tender heart. Did she spurn with her little foot the dead leopard, that had stolen the fawn?"

"She did!"

"Would Ameena spurn those who stole Hoossein?"

"No one stole him; he was drowned."

"Who told you so?"

"Yusuff."

"Did Ameena weep?"

"Ameena does not recollect."

"Ameena has a good memory; she recollects the things of more than thirty years ago, yet she forgets if she wept when her betrothed was drowned; she did not weep then; her heart had changed, and she does not now recollect her oldest friend."

"Are you Hoossein?" gasped Ameena.

"I am! Look here," and he showed her a talisman, with which in her childhood she had loved to play.

"Yes," she said, "it was his, but they told me he was dead."

"For all you cared he was!"

"Have you risen again to torment me?" said Ameena. "I never intentionally injured you, I was told that you had gone. I was ordered to marry Ibrahim."

"Will Ameena tell me how he died?"

"I will," she said, "if you do not frighten me, but it is easier to say I remember things when brought to my notice, than to recall circumstances which are not mentioned; the fact I know, but the details are dim before me. He died,—yes!—he died in the water!"

"Was he drowned?"

"Oh no!"

"What killed him?"

"He died!"

"Of what?"

"Oh! do not speak like that; you did not speak roughly when you brought the honey. He died. Yes, he was ill with fever, and he had to get water for the men, then there was some one there, and Ibrahim fell down, and I found him there, and he died!"

"Did some one kill him?"

"Oh, no!"

"What did he die of, then?"

"Oh! do not frighten me, Hoossein!"

"Who was there?"

"No one."

"You just said that some one was there; who was it?"

"Oh yes! he came after—"

"Did he kill Ibrahim?"

"He kill him? Oh no! he never did harm to any one but himself. I wanted to die, too. I remember all now: he would not let me die, but he took me away, and called the doctor. Then they went to bury Ibrahim; but the river had risen, and Ibrahim had gone away with it."

"I was told," said Hossein, "that the Saheb had killed him for your sake."

"I was told," retorted Ameena, "that you were dead; and that is not so great a lie as the other. The young Hoossein believed in Ameena; he is dead. The old Hoossein does not believe in her or anyone else. He kill Ibrahim? What for! No, no! Eglington Saheb loved everyone, and everyone loved him."

"You did not spurn him then as you did the leopard that stole your pet fawn?"

"Hoossein Saheb! he did not steal my fawn; he did not ask for my love; he was kind, and he was good; he nursed me in my madness, as if I had been his sister. The water was cold, and my head was hot. I was ill, very ill. I did not know myself. I was on the road to the unknown world. I awoke, with that rough world before me, cold and dreary. It was the Saheb poured the dew of heaven on my parched lips. I thought he was an angel, sent to meet me at the gates. Would not you, Hoossein, have loved an angel? And then the Saheb was ill, and I nursed him; and so he loved me. We loved one another. But he died two years ago, and left me with two daughters. I am now on my way to Calcutta."

"Alone?" asked Hoossein.

"I am alone now; but a Saheb awaits me there."

"I thought so," lisped Hoossein. "You have become a Christian woman; and you live with the Christian man."

"I am not a Christian. No one has ever tried to convert me. I have never forgotten my faith. Eglington, Saheb said to me, 'Go on in the religion you were brought up in. Adhere to the faith of your fathers, through all trials, and all temptations. If you lightly reject that for an earthly love, you will be like a ship at sea without a rudder; you will toss about where the waves throw you, and know not right from wrong. But,' he said, "if at any time you feel a conviction that your creed is wrong, that it leads you into error—that you neglect your God, reject his precepts, and do ill to your neighbour—then, if you wish it, I will consult those who are learned in the subject, and thank my Saviour if it leads to good.' I felt, Hoossein Saheb, that this was right. I have tried to do my duty to my neighbours, and to fulfil my destiny with thankfulness."

" Did the Saheb teach you this ?" asked Hoossein.

" He did ; and a great deal more of good."

" If all had been like him, we should not be about to kill them," whispered Hoossein.

" Kill whom ?" said Ameena, in alarm.

" Be silent! all the Feringhis."

" You kill them all ? You are mad, Hoossein—you have been mad from your childhood—they all said you were mad, when you killed the leopard. You cannot kill them ; you do not know how numerous they are—as soon as one goes, two come in his place. You must not try to kill them."

" We shall kill them all, and rule this country ; we will do our own people good, and make all followers of the Prophet."

" You should not trust me with this," said Ameena ; "I am bound by the strongest ties of gratitude to the English—to the ladies in particular; they nursed me when I was ill, and fed me when I was hungry, and clothed me when I was naked. Sit down, Hoossein, and listen to me; I have a long tale to tell you. I am to go on in the morning, so I must tell you now, if you will listen."

So they sat down on the carpet.

"You remember me, Hoossein, a merry, thoughtless child. I could laugh at joy and smile at sorrow. My first serious affliction was that you sent me no message for me to follow you when I thought you were gone; night after night I sent my little light afloat on the waters to guide you back, but you never saw my star. Will you do so now?

"When Yusuff came home and told us of your death, I was persuaded to marry Ibrahim; but I was not happy for some time—I thought I had done wrong—then the feeling wore away. He was very good to me; I obeyed him, attended to him, and thought it very cruel that I was not allowed to go away with him. You, Hoossein, first taught me to accept my destiny, whatever it might be, but there was much to endure—captivity, cold, and hunger. I alone ministered to the prisoners, because I was a Mahomedan. I conveyed to them news from the outer world; the guards searched me daily, but they got careless when they found nothing—one day a Saheb upset the ink bottle; the guard heard it, and we all expected to be executed, but I was suddenly seized with a fit, and, sitting down on the ink, I wiped it up with my dress, and I felt I had done a good thing, and saved many lives of the good and brave. I was so happy at being able to do good, and a daughter was born in my captivity; then, through the kindness of Mahomedans, we escaped, through frost and snow, over pathless mountains and raging streams. Eglington Saheb was advised to leave me and our child to our fates; his duty required of him to leave us; but he said that I had been entrusted to him, and while life lasted he would be true to his trust. So in the end we got back to his own people, and we lived a quiet life, and another daughter was born; they both sleep in that room. We are here on our way to Calcutta, where a great and a good man is to meet us; you must not kill him—he is so good; if you knew these people as I do, you would not wish to kill them. You do not know how they work for your good; they educate us; they shew us all useful things; they are very wise. I thought my father, Yusuff, was a wise man, but he was like a little child compared with the white men; they know all the stars of Heaven and all the regions of the world; they travel from one end of the world to the other by the aid of boiling water; they talk in an unheard language all round the world, they get the sun to paint pictures for them; and you, who know nothing of all these wonders, think that you can destroy them. Wisdom is power, Hoossein! When you know more, you will either be unwilling to injure them, or you will be unable to do it."

" All they do, all they think of is, to destroy caste, and to pervert our religions," said Hoossein.

"Nonsense!" said Ameena; " they will never interfere with one or the other; a few may talk of religion, and some may talk of caste, but that is no reason why we should bear animosity to those who do not. I have heard our own people say that caste prejudices do more harm than good; if this is true, we should be grateful to the English for breaking down the system, but, unfortunately for your theory, the English have rather confirmed caste rights, by granting every request founded on them; and now that there is no more to ask for on that plea, they are asking for greater things. And you, Hoossein, are one of that party; you were one of those who joined with the men who refused to work at Mooltan; who eat the salt of, but refused the work, of the masters; who reviled the Bombay soldiers, because they performed a soldier's duty and obeyed their masters. Are you,

Hoossein, one of those who sympathised with the men who, calling themselves troopers, refused to follow their officers to the charge at Modkee? If so, you cannot be the Hoossein I knew—he was bright and chivalrous; as such, I was taught to look up to him as the first, most excellent man on earth. But you are not the old friend—you are a new man. Tell me, Hoossein, from whence did you get this impulse to murder?"

"It is my destiny," was the reply; "it will be accomplished. The black people on the other side of the world have done it, and so will we do it; they live in ease and enjoyment, while we are slaves to these English, and find it difficult to live amidst plenty; they are tyrants, Ameena; they rob us, they consume us."

"No! no!" cried Ameena; "they do not rob you—they are no tyrants; look at the Mahomedans—were they tyrants, when they killed hundreds of thousands on the score of religion? were the Hindoos tyrants when they laid waste whole regions for a similar purpose? Talk of destiny, indeed!—there is no destiny in it, till the thing is done. A Mahomedan must not follow him on whom there is an everlasting curse; it is in our Koran, Hoossein; the African is a 'servant of servants,' the very scum of the earth, and you would follow his base example and murder those who do you good. Do not disgrace our creed by doing this."

"It is done, Ameena; it is written in this scroll: 'What thou doest, do.' The waters are already overflowing—the flood is rolling on; look to thyself, Ameeña! I came but to warn you—depart from hence; it is an unsafe place for any one who befriends the English; there are those at hand who will respect neither sex or age of those who befriend the white man."

"I go!" said Ameena.

"Go!" said Hoossein.

And thus the oldest friends parted—one to make preparations for the slaughter of, the other to warn the English of their danger.

CHAPTER XVIII.

THE TREE WITH ONE BOUGH.

It was a strong dam, carefully prepared; it had stood the storms of many years, but now came a flood trickling over the top, and sapping the foundation below; its strength was of no avail—a large breach was made; there was a spring of evil in itself, and now the foaming torrent poured through, raging and boiling; the embankments gave way, and the broken fragments were hurried on to mix with the sediment of things departed, to be lost in the chaotic mass of mixtures never again to be recognised as portions of what they once had been—never again to be heard of as bits of the Bengal Sepoy Army, but still to be found by the curious, mixed up with the soil of the earth.

Stealthily, almost unnoticed, quite ignored, the flood had gathered a strong head; no wonder, when the spring undermined the foundation, that the structure fell. Fractures and rents had been badly repaired: the superintendent refused to credit the bad condition of the building; his employers believed his assertions, that all was right; there were clumsy workmen about, lax, unskilled, and given to other occupations. The masonry was soft, the cement unadhesive, so the work gave way, astonishing only the head man and his employers.

The storm was awful; there were fire balls falling from the heavens, meteors glaring over the earth, and dusky red patches of flickering light on the far horizon.

Hoossein was alarmed as he strode out into the night. There were signs of the end of the world, and the question that had of late more than once been put to him, rose in its phantom shape before him, blue and ghastly,

"Who are you who try to control us?" were words replied to with sarcasm, ridicule, or reason—depending on the circle from which the question came; but when his own conscience asked him the question alone in the darkness, there was another reply, "Who am I?"

Hoossein answered himself, "No one!" He felt that all was lost, yet he said to himself as he stepped hastily along towards the uproar and the din, "I may do something yet."

As Hoossein gathered a few of his followers together, a confused noise sounded in his ear; the flash of fire arms fell upon his eye; there were flickering flames and crackling timber, crashing falls and clouds of dust;] he met some running from, and others passed him, running to the scene of confusion.

The Sepoy lines were all in flames, the bungalows of the officers were fiercely blazing, crowds of men were around them, and the sounds were as if Jehannum had sent out its legions of evil for the occasion.

Here and there, across the clear, open parade ground, white people had escaped, pursued by a rabble of black men; there were little knots of men collected here and there to witness, 'neath the glaring light of their own houses, the last indignities practised by fiendish tormentors on the overtaken runaways.

The lurid glare was dying away as Hoossein came upon the scene; there was no more matter to burn, no more life to destroy. There was a tinge of grey light in the east, but the atmosphere was murky; it smelled of smoke and the funeral pile.

Through all this the surging, yelling masses ran; the chase was up; there was more to be done in the city, so on they ran, roaring like tigers, howling like wolves; they were not contented with simple death, they hacked, they tore, they tormented. There were hissing of flames, the screams of the tortured, and roars of laughter; men demanding death, women imploring to be killed; and midst all this, there lay the mutilated bodies of little white children. The reality of the scene surpassed even Hoossein's ideas of horror, and almost eclipsed his desire of vengeance, but on he went with the roaring crowd.

Rapine and plunder were all the fashion. Feringhis had been concealed by friends; houses were ransacked, the inmates were ill treated, a chaotic confusion reigned. His worst fears were realised; zeal and order were confounded, like the confused waves of a troubled sea. Wickedness overthrew order, as the salt tide rolls up the river; the efforts made to stop its current were like a child's sand heap on the margin of the ocean—like a lump of clay endeavouring to turn the stream of molten lava from the volcano.

Hoossein had added "Bahadoor" to his

name, but it gave him no authority over those at a distance, or over those whom he did not pay. Before this night he had travelled far and fast; he had argued, he had coaxed, and threatened; he was abused, and called a coward; he condescended to explain many times. "Wait for the waters to help us —wait and live; be impatient and die!"

His arguments were all lost; his title did not impose on the furious Hydra. Its blood was up, there was no guider, and at last a panic seized on all. Religion, caste, pride, jealousy, rapacity, insubordination, contempt, and fear contended with hesitation, inability, economy, faith, patience, fortitude, and religion; all but the three last gave way before the storm.

Now the prison doors were opened. In liberating the prisoners, an accumulated mass of evil was sluiced out on the unfortunate locality. Years and years of cooped up unforgotten sin revelled again in unforgotten liberty. The murderer, the dacoit, the burglar, the torturer, the child robber, and the petty thieves, all intelligent in their vocation, acquiring more dexterity than the ordinary routine of life requires, all more eager for indulgence from long restraint, more delighted from unexpected and forcible liberation, all rushed unbridled on the scene.

"What a scene," thought Hoossein, to himself, as he sought in vain to find a ringleader to this miserable outbreak, "and into this scene are accidentally thrown the only beings upon earth whom I should wish to be far away—one, my unseen, my unacknowledged daughter; the other, my betrothed. I have saved the former, now for the latter. Yusuff's dream is coming true."

As he passed along he was suddenly aware of a palanquin turning up a side street; the door was open, and to his astonishment he recognised Tara.

"Where are you going?" he asked.

"There was danger, so I came back; I am safe now!"

Hoossein was aware of an armed guard, but he said,

"There is danger everywhere; where is Soultan?"

"Gone to look for you; Ameena wants you. There are your people yelling about the house!"

"The floods are let loose," said Hoossein. "Wait for me at the Musjeed," and he hurried on to the house which he had left only a few hours before.

As he approached the place, there was a crash, as of a hundred guns firing at once; round about was a crowd of people, of all sorts, all castes, and all creeds; men who so lately cavilled about minute questions and caste privileges, mingled all together, rushing on for one common object. There were houses to be plundered, mischief to be done, and people to be murdered.

Burning houses threw a lurid light on the morning dawn, casting unncertain lights on the heated and frantic demons at their work of destruction. On they surged, with fierce yells, to a tall house. Flames issued from the windows, smoke issued from the door-way, shrieks were heard within, screaming and the wailing of women in distress. There was to be no mercy; they were English, or the friends of the English.

It was a scene of utter confusion. The dust and smoke rendered things indistinct; the early light and lurid flames shone for a moment through the smoke in the door-way. One glance was sufficient.

Ameena, his youthful friend, was struggling with the fiends; she was imploring pity for herself and children. They were all true Mahomedans. At that moment she saw Hoossein.

"Oh, save us! save us!" she cried.

A few followers were still around Hoossein. He required their aid to rescue true Mahomedans. Then, without waiting to see if he was obeyed, he rushed on, crying,

"I am Hoossein Bahadoor."

He plunged his dagger to the hilt in the back of a man, who was holding Ameena's hair to the ground; then, drawing a pistol, he shot a ruffian, who had held her hands. She was liberated, and placed under protection. The daughters were not to be found. The smoke, thick and suffocating, issued from within, and screams of agony were heard.

While endeavouring to find an entrance into these rooms by a back door, Hoossein was aware of a volley of musketry; then he heard the measured tread of military, and turning round he saw that he was surrounded by a party of English soldiers, who took his arms from him, and led him away.

"I thought how it would be," thought Hoossein. "Those idiots, straining at a gnat, have swallowed the camel, priding themselves on their high caste. They are now contaminated with the lowest of the low, and with all manner of abominations. This comes of working with those who act solely on their own passions; men who, taking service as soldiers, could never submit to discipline; men serving a people who, as Sambo said, were too intent on their own gains, pleasures, or idleness, to control those whom accident had placed under their rule ; a people who, instead of making religion their starting point, impressing every one with its importance, try to govern other creeds without it, to influence all classes by moral power without a standard of morality, themselves living in utter disregard of it. Yes! what could I expect, but chaos and confusion?"

There was but little time for thought. The party hurried on with several prisoners; the gates of the old city were passed. A long line of troops was drawn up on the plain beyond. Hoossein looked towards the Musjeed, that place in which he had so often excited the admiration of the spectators, by his devout behaviour, his elegant prostrations, and his neat carpet. He passed close by it, and he looked on this place of prayer and meeting; standing near it was a bullock gharee, with white bullocks; there was also a palanquin; a native female stood by it, unveiled, with Europeans beside her. They were talking of him, and the woman Tara laughed.

The spirit of helpless wrath raged within him. Soultan was there; he called on that faithful friend to aid him, as he attempted to escape. Soultan never acknowledged the request.

Hoossein was overpowered, handcuffs were put on him. Pinioned, beaten, and wounded, compelled to go on, with a bayonet touching his back, he turned round for one more look. There was a smile, but no pity upon Tara's face.

The bitterness of death rushed over Hoossein's frame, as the pestilential blast destroys the herbage of the field. In a moment he was a broken man, and shook like the leaf that falls before the breeze. He thought that he deserved to die for many things that he had done, but not for what had happened that morning.

Hoossein, with several other prisoners, was led up to a large tent, to await their trial. A drum stood before it; round the drum sat several officers—one a grey-haired, calm old man, who seemed deeply impressed with the solemnity of his duty. One by one, or in small parties, the prisoners were tried, and led off. Many of them were cavalry men, Mahomedans, some of whom recognised Hoossein, who understood that they were to be blown away from the artillery guns, a number of which stood unlimbered near.

Hoossein was brought up the last of all. The accusation against him was, that he had that morning killed two men.

The white-haired Englishman asked him his name.

" Hoossein Ben Hassan," he replied.

" Hoossein Ben Hassan was in my service twenty-eight years ago, at ——. Are you the same ?"

" I am."

" Go on, Provost Marshal."

"This man, Hoossein Saheb, as he is commonly called, was seen this morning to stab one man, who was picked up dead. He also shot another, who is here, and likely to die. Hoossein Saheb is notorious about the native camps, as an owner of divans and houses of bad fame. His houses have been the resort of the evil-disposed for many years; his haunts have been at Agra, Delhi, at Dum Dum, Barrackpoor, Moorshedebad, Lucknow, and Bareilly. He has been heard of at Mooltan and Lahore; a native woman, one Ailee, can give evidence regarding him extending over many years."

"Is this charge true?" asked the president.

"It is," said Hoossein, "but I killed the man this morning because he was injuring a woman."

"Hang him as a murderer!" was the only reply.

Hoossein Ben Hassan was turned round. At the distance of a few yards stood a tree;

from a bough, denuded of its leaves and branches, dangled a rope.

The prisoner walked towards it with a haughty air, and a firm step. He placed himself beneath the noose. As it was adjusted round his neck, he said, with a smile, in his last breath,

"I have fulfilled my destiny! 'What thou doest do!' Here is the tree with the one bough."

THE END.

www.ingramcontent.com/pod-product-compliance
Lightning Source LLC
Chambersburg PA
CBHW030803230426
43667CB00008B/1043